LITICAL

20° Greenwich
30°
40°
50°
TURKEY
Athens
Cyprus (Brit.)
Crete
Urfa
Euphrates
Mosul
Tigris
Tehran
Aleppo
SYRIA
Beirut
Damascus
Baghdad
IRAQ
IRA
Port Said
Alexandria
PAL
Jerusalem
TR. JORDAN
CAIRO
Suez
Aqaba
Jauf
Basra
Shuster
Shiraz
Neutral
PERSIAN GULF
Siwa
el Faiyum
Aujila
Hail
Bandar Abbas
Bahrein
Farafra
Asyut
Kena
EGYPT
SAUDI
Medina
El Kharga
Aswan
Hejaz
RED SEA
TRUCIAL
OMAN
ARABIA
Mecca
Halfa
Jiddah
Bardai
P. Sudan
Suakin
Dongola
Atbara
ANGLO-EGYPTIAN
Omdurman
Khartoum
Kassala
Massowa
Sana
YEMEN
ERITREA
Adua
ADEN PROT.
to Bombay 1650
Abeshe
El Fasher
El Obeid
Gondar
Assab
Aden (Brit.)
Sokotra (Brit.)
SUDAN
G. of ADEN
C. Guardafui
Jibuti
Zeila
Berbera
Kodok (Fashoda)
Addis Ababa
BRIT. SOMALILD.
Harar
ABYSSINIA (ETHIOPIA)
EQUATORIAL AFRICA
Obbia
ITALIAN SOMALILAND
Bejaf
Wadelai
Bardera
Mogadiscio
1720
R. Congo
UGANDA
KENYA
Coquilhatville
Stanleyville
Jinja
Kisumu
Ponthierville
Entebbe
Lake Victoria
Nairobi
Kismayu
to Goa 2340
BELGIAN CONGO
Lamu
INDIAN
Kindu
TANGANYIKA
Mombasa
British Mandated
Pemba I.
P. Francqui
Ujiji
Tabora
Bagamoyo
ZANZIBAR
Amirante Is. Brit.
Lake Tanganyika
TERRITORY
Dar es Salaam
OCEAN
Kilwa
Aldabra Brit.
Providence I.
Bukama
Lindi
Kambove
Comoro (Fr.)
GOLA
553
Lake Nyasa
NYASALAND
MOZAMBIQUE
Nossi Be
NORTHERN RHODESIA
Lusaka
Mozambique
MADAGASCAR
Livingstone
Zambezi
Tete
Blantyre
SOUTHERN RHODESIA
Salisbury
Sena
Quilimane
Chinde
485
Tamatave
Antananarivo
Mauritius (Brit.)
Beira
Sofala
Bulawayo
Reunion (Fr.)
TH WEST
BECHUANALAND
Windhoek
RICA
Europa I.
Tulia
475
Inhambane
1344
TRANSVAAL
JOHANNESBURG
Pretoria
Lourenço Marques
Delagoa B.
P. Dauphin
C. Ste. Marie
UNION OF
Kimberley
ORANGE FREE STATE
NATAL
Durban to Tamatave
to Mauritius 1552
INDIAN
Bloemfontein
B.A.S.
Pietermaritzburg
Durban
SOUTH AFRICA
CAPE OF GOOD HOPE
253
OCEAN
East London
P. Elizabeth
420
131
Cape Town to Melbourne 5814, to Hobart 5838
30°
40°
50°
60°
20°
10°
0°

BEFORE THE WIND OF CHANGE

BEFORE THE WIND OF CHANGE

by

W. T. C. Berry, CBE, MA, MD, DTM & H

Former Principal Medical Officer (Nutrition), Department of Health
& Social Security and previously Medical Officer,
Colonial Medical Service, Nyasaland & Gambia, 1936-1948

This work was completed by W. T. C. Berry before his death in July 1983 and was prepared for publication by Veronica Berry

ISBN 0 950 9470 0 8

All proceeds from the sale of this book will go to
The Chest, Heart & Stroke Association
Tavistock House
North Tavistock Square
London WC1H 9JE

The Halesworth Press, Suffolk, England

In memory
of 43 years of happy marriage

William Thomas Charles Berry, aged 27

CONTENTS

LIST OF ILLUSTRATIONS

Page

ACKNOWLEDGEMENTS TO:

Our son, Tom, and to Iris and John, our daughter and son-in-law, who encouraged my husband's efforts at writing his recollections of Africa after his stroke, until, from having 'nothing to say' he gradually became aware that there was much he wanted to write and that they wanted to read.

My cousin, A. E. Gunther, for much practical advice.

Mrs Joyce Doughty, late of the London School of Hygiene and Tropical Medicine, who dealt with our enquiries with such kindly patience.

R. W. Kettlewell, R. Keppel-Compton, H. J. H. Borley and Mrs Mae Cran, who bore with our questions, cudgelled their brains and came up with their recollections of times long past.

'Jabe', (Mrs Jessie Williamson), who lent us her private papers and photographs.

Dr T. P. Eddy, and to 'The Dietician', 'The Administrator' and 'The Mechanic' who all provided useful information.

The London School of Hygiene and Tropical Medicine for lending the Nyasaland Survey and Nutrition Development Unit papers of 1938-43.

Dr Sylvia Darke who cleared up a puzzling medical point for me in the MS.

Malcolm Howard, FMPA, FSAI, MIRT, LRPS, FRSA, who photographed unpromising material with such success.

Stephen Taylor of Queen Mary College, for his sketch map of the swamp and villages surrounding Genieri in the Gambia.

To all, my very grateful thanks.

Veronica Berry
March 1984

Foreword

'An *ignis fatuus* that bewitches, and lures men into bogs and ditches.' So runs the couplet. From the age of 27 to 38 I sought, increasingly, in Central and in West Africa, the Will-o'-the-Wisp of genuine self-rule for Africa, only leaving off because I had to, and only pausing to look objectively at myself when, at the age of 72, I had a stroke. This left me partly immobilised, with time on my hands, and with the knowledge that my days were done. Even so, I would never have written the account had it not been for my wife with her sympathetic interest (and the letters which she had kept from those far off days), and had it not been for the insistence of my children, to whom my reminiscences of Africa revealed a strange — and past — world which was quite contrary to their impressions of Empire as related by the 'media' during their lifetime.

The first part of this story is therefore a light-hearted young man's impressions of Africa in the Colonial Medical Service before the second World War, when air travel was in its infancy and letters from home took six weeks to arrive by sea mail. The second part is more serious, more disillusioned, as the *'ignis fatuus'* is pursued in vain.

It is said that an observant Bantu chief, summarising the way of approach of the British Empire, remarked: 'First the missionary, then the trader, then the gunboat.' I was concerned with none of these, but it was in the spirit of the first that I went to practise medicine in the Colonial Medical Service. My mother was a Theosophist and her beliefs appealed more to my senses of logic and justice than did the major faiths with their emphasis on a single physical life and on the importance of the particular faith which they proffer as essential to eternal salvation. I was never a trader, but the need for the commercial development of Africa was forced upon me by my experience with the Bantu and led me to dabble in farm mechanisation, particularly its development as a means of strengthening, rather than weakening, the structure of African society and of the need to introduce it in a form capable of being adapted to meet and master the stresses of commercialisation. I never served on a gunboat but my efforts to leave the Colonial Service and join the Navy at the outbreak of war will be described in due course. In short, I lived perforce as a spectator in the world of missionary, trader and gunboat, or something like it, in the Empire, and now, with time to think and to recall, I present this version of my days in Africa to my children and grand-children.

INTRODUCTION

I was born in Tunbridge Wells, Kent, on May 4th 1909, the second of three sons. My father, Charles Berry, came from Curry Rivel in Somerset, the fourth son in a family of seven sons and two daughters.

My grandfather, Thomas Darby Berry, an estate agent, was the son of Thomas Berry (1804-1873) and Ann Darby (1810-1853), and grandson of Thomas Berry (1767-1807), of Hartley Row, Hampshire, and Catherine Editha Fulmer of London.

My grandmother, Louisa Mary Berry, (1848-1926), was the daughter of Robert Sewers (1806-1873) of Curry Rivel, Somerset. Her mother, Mary Ann Bayley, the daughter of a calico printer living at Broughton in the County of Lancaster, married a merchant of Everton, John Holmes, in 1844, and the child, Louisa Mary, born in 1848 at Eastham, in the County of Chester, was registered as Louisa Mary Holmes. The father's name, however, does not appear on the Birth Certificate and Robert Sewers, in his Will, dated 1869, referred to her as his 'natural daughter', Louisa Mary, the wife of Thomas Darby Berry.

Robert Sewers, himself, was one of the thirteen children born to Elizabeth, the adopted daughter of Robert (1707-1795) and Martha Keetch, and to Philip Sewers (1752-1831) her husband, of Ashby-de-la-Zouche. One of Robert's elder sisters was a milliner in London and one of his brothers a trunkmaker. Robert appears to have married a French girl, Clélie Aland, mentioned in the milliner's diary, sometime in the eighteen thirties, but she does not figure in the family records so the marriage may have been short-lived.

My father became a lawyer and after a spell with a London firm, Williams & James, moved to Tunbridge Wells in 1906 as junior partner to a Mr Elvey Robb. They were joined in 1914 by a Mr Welch and the firm became Robb, Berry & Welch, an unfortunate combination which gave rise to cynical comment in the town. Welch was killed in the First World War and Robb decided to practice in London, while still retaining the right to a third of the profits in Tunbridge Wells. He then began approaching Tunbridge Wells' clients to persuade them to consult him in London, so obtaining the full fees. My father decided to buy him out for £1000, but when a meeting took place Robb refused to sign the prepared document. In high dudgeon my father knocked him down and when Robb arose, very indignant, he knocked him down again, whereupon the document was signed without further comment. When my elder brother, Richard Steven, joined my father in 1930 the name of the firm became Berry & Berry and remained so when my younger brother, James Ivor, entered the partnership in 1935.

My father started in rooms above the National Provincial Bank, 89, Mount Pleasant, later moving to 15 Church Road. Berry & Berry remained in Church Road, moving to No. 11; No. 13 was acquired after the Second World War. In 1930, besides the two partners, the staff consisted of two managing clerks, my father's invaluable secretary, Miss Holmes, who remained with the firm until she retired, four typists and two office boys. Today, (1982) it consists of five partners, two assistant solicitors, three legal executives, two articled pupils, two accountants, thirteen typists and two receptionists.

In 1903 my father married Alice Lilian Nott, one of a family of five girls and one boy. Alice Nott's great-grandfather was born in Neath, South Wales, in 1783, the son of Charles Nott (said to be an innkeeper) and Mary Bailey. He rose to be Major General Sir William Nott of Kandahar and Shawl, gaining his title and honours in the first Afghan War of 1841.

In 1805 he married Letitia Swinhoe by whom he had 14 children, only seven of whom survived to maturity. His third son, Robert Murray Nott, had four children, the eldest son, Robert McIntosh Nott (1847-1889), being Alice's father.

Robert McIntosh Nott joined the 2nd Dublin Fusiliers, and married a Mary Louisa Leatherbarough, who, between 1876 and 1887, gave birth to seven children. In 1889, while the Regiment was stationed in Gibraltar, both parents died, Robert in July, aged 42, his wife in September, aged 40, together with their eldest daughter, Cora Rose, aged 13. The family was then split up and the children adopted by various philanthropic couples, Alice and her sister, Violet, by a rich, childless couple named Cleasby, Mrs Cleasby looking forward to their companionship in her old age if they did not marry. Her plans went awry as such plans do, when Violet fell in love with an Army officer, Charles Kitchin, and his school friend, Charles Berry, (not in the Army but in the law, only a degree more highly regarded than 'trade' in those days) fell in love with Alice and she with him. Violet's engagement was sanctioned but Alice was banned from seeing Charles, until her health suffered to such a degree that Mr Cleasby relented (Mrs Cleasby being away at the time) and they were allowed to marry. Mrs Cleasby never forgave her, however, and she inherited little or nothing of the Cleasby's considerable fortune.

The young couple went through a lean time in the early part of their married life while my father built up his solicitor's practice. My brothers and I were born in 1904, 1909 and 1910 and during and after these years my parents moved house several times in and around Tunbridge Wells. In order to increase his capital, my father began to experiment in, and thereby gain experience of, the property market: he would buy a house going cheaply for some reason, move into it and on its defects thus becoming apparent, he and my mother would decide how to improve it. Having made the improvement, often a quite simple alteration which had prevented its sale before, he sold the house again. By doing this my father became a very shrewd judge of the property market.

Christening of *Philip Berry*, c. 1878. *Maid, Guy, Philip,* in *nurse's* arms.
Louisa Mary Berry, Charles (aged 2) Ethel, Bob, Darby.

Charles Berry (1876-1942) Guernsey 1928

Major General Sir William Nott of Kandahar and Shawl (1783-1845)

XV

Alice Lilian Berry (née Nott) c. 1928 (1879-1970)

Richard Steven, James Ivor, William Thomas Charles c.1911

After being rejected five times for military service in the early years of the 1914-18 war because of an old knee injury, he was eventually accepted towards the end of the war and served in the 4th Sussex Regiment in England. On demobilisation he came back to the practice and we moved to 16, Molyneux Park, in Tunbridge Wells. It was a typical Edwardian family house and garden and was run with the two servants, a cook-general and a house parlourmaid, considered indispensable by middle-class families. 'Cookie' (Miss Edith Summers), the sharp-tongued but devoted mainstay of the house, remained with the family for years and was eventually provided with a pension by my father; the houseparlour-maids changed fairly frequently.

In 1937 when we had all left the parental roof — my brothers were married and I was by then in Africa — the house was sold and my parents moved into a smaller house, Mount Edgcumbe Cottage, on the edge of the Common in Tunbridge Wells. They were there when Hitler's war broke out and my father died there in 1942. In 1946 the house went to my brother Richard and his wife, and my mother began a somewhat peripatetic life until her death some twenty years later.

Early in her married life my mother became deeply involved with Theosophy, which she found gave her the purpose which had been lacking in her trivial daily round at the Cleasbys. From her first introduction to Theosophy her life was 'quite literally changed' (her actual words) and though my father was not enthusiastic about unorthodox religion, his affection for my mother and his great respect for her clear, logical brain mellowed his attitude to her Theosophical beliefs. She went on, eventually, to become General Secretary of the Theosophical Society and visited the Theosophical headquarters in India, when she spent some months there after the war.

A child's place in the family can be a major influence governing his behaviour. I was a middle son with an elder brother, Dick, four years older than myself and a younger brother, Jim, only fifteen months younger, treading hard on my heels all through my schooldays. Both brothers grew up larger and stronger than myself, more good-looking and more successful with girls. Dick won many prizes at school and both brothers were better at Rugger. In comparison I regarded myself as a 'weed', being much slighter in build, very short-sighted and shy. I spent my early life striving to do as well as Dick and to keep ahead of Jim, in spheres unsuited to me (I was too short-sighted to be a good Rugger player) and in later life was constantly driven by the urge to excel. But success persistently eluded me — or I thought it did. For example, from Eversley Preparatory School in the Frant Road, I tried for a scholarship to Tonbridge. This I failed to get but passed out top of the candidates for entrance with Jim coming second, on my heels as usual! But my success was marred for me because I was at the upper age limit and it was considered *only natural* that I should come top, whereas Jim was at the lower age limit and therefore deemed to have done very well to pass at all!

I disliked my years at Tonbridge as a day boy. The drain on my parents' purse of educating three sons at public school and University, made boarding out of the question and in any event was not looked on with favour by my mother. For economic reasons day boys were of humbler origin than boarders and this did nothing to alleviate my innate sense of inferiority. In a large public school the proportion of day boys was small and in those days they were almost uniformly looked down on. Tonbridge had a reputation for 'toughness' and, as at many public schools, prowess at games was esteemed above scholarship. I recollect that on, I think, Skinners' Day, when the Governors of the School paid us a visit, they were formally welcomed by the Head Boy who read a speech to them entirely in Latin. We boys were informed in advance that when he raised his voice in tone for a few words or phrases this signified that a Latin joke was being told, and we all, Governors and pupils alike, broke into forced laughter. The Captains of the First XV and of cricket were regarded as 'God's Younger Brother Alf' as the saying used to be, and in my time a day boy never rose to such celestial heights.

Nor was my time at Cambridge a particularly happy one; here, I was less successful with the other sex than my contemporaries. Dick went to Gonville and Caius College because it was known as a 'rowing College' and he had rowed at Tonbridge. It was also a 'medical' College so I naturally followed him, and Jim followed me. I do not remember when, or even if, I made the conscious choice to

William Thomas Charles Berry James Ivor Berry
Richard Steven Berry 1935

become a doctor — my mother maintained that by the age of five I was interested in insects and plants and that it was obvious that I had a scientific bent. No doubt my father reckoned that the business, though successful, might be hard stretched to support three sons, and that a doctor had a better chance than other scientists, such as botanists or entomologists, so steered me, not unwillingly, towards a medical career. My parents hoped that I would eventually set up my plate in Tunbridge Wells and it was a very bitter blow to them when I later joined the Colonial Medical Service.

I was always interested in the practical aspects of doctoring so that when I entered St. Bartholomew's Medical School in 1930 I really began to enjoy my work and, as a result, my life — perhaps also the fact that I was no longer in competition with my brothers had something to do with it, though I went into the world with prickly sensitivities which would have delighted any psychiatrist. One's merit as a clinician, however, is accurately conveyed by one's colleagues who are also 'walking the wards'. Here I was regarded as 'a good sound man' not, that is, among the brilliant few who were destined to become consultants, but likely to be among the reliable but not specially distinguished general practitioners who today are the backbone of the National Health Service.

My companions were mainly public school boys who came from comfortable homes and an incident remains in my memory which brought home to me the wretchedness of the Britain in which we lived, unconscious or too little conscious of our surroundings in the security of our middleclass fathers' earnings. On Bart's district — the area of Islington and the slums around — we callow students learnt through practical experience the art and science of obstetrics and midwifery. I had just completed the task of ushering a fifth baby into a bug-ridden house, and I asked the mother if she would like a drink of water. 'Yes', she said, 'that's our cup on the shelf there.' One cup! between five children and two parents!

After passing our finals in 1933, two friends and I decided to have one last glorious fling before going 'into bondage' and we spent over two months climbing in Norway, then crossing Lapland and making our way down Sweden on foot, camping on the way. On my return I served among the housemen at Barts and in provincial hospitals and at St. Andrew's Hospital, Dollis Hill, I was fortunate enough to work under Sir Harold Gillies, the plastic surgeon. I was then for some months an assistant to two hard-pressed doctors in a coal mining area in the Midlands. What I saw there of panel practice almost put me off doctoring for life. The older partner once said: 'All you need for success in a place like this is a glib tongue and a nose for danger', completely discounting the fact that he worked immensely hard and long hours and that his mere presence at the bedside improved the patient's morale. The younger partner said: 'You were quite right about that child with urticaria when you told the parents that it would clear up completely in a matter of hours without treatment, but when you left they called me personally and I came out and prescribed some medicine *"to purify the blood"'!* I learnt a lot with them but the life, under grey and weeping skies, in drab surroundings and with pathetically inadequate means of improving the health of my patients, together with a bad bout of 'flu, depressed me.

Paradoxically, the very inadequacy of our powers stimulated us to greater effort: 'You can leave a patient, thinking that you have done everything that can be done for him but that is not enough', said the elder partner, 'you must think again and something may occur to you. But that too is not enough, when you wake in the night you must think again and eventually you will have thought of everything.' And this for the lean rewards that then came from panel practice.

NYASALAND PROTECTORATE.

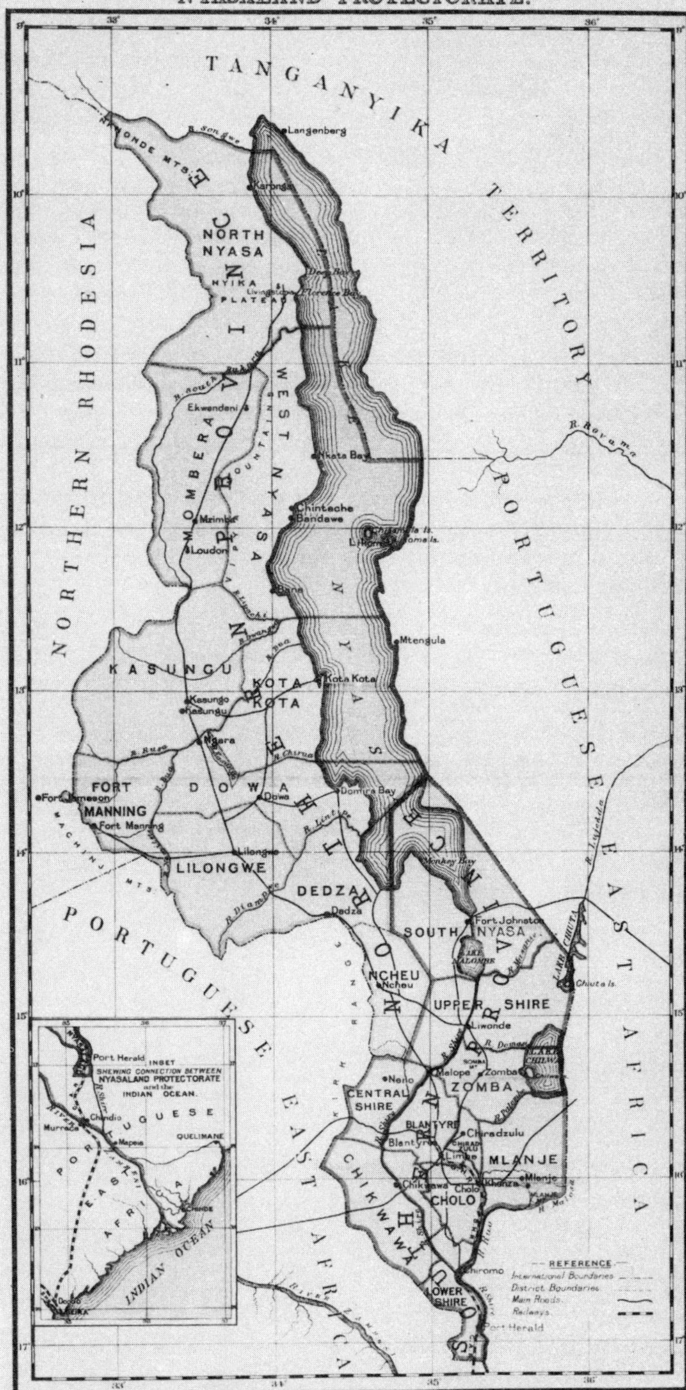

ELEVATION ABOVE SEA LEVEL OF PRINCIPAL PLACES (APPROXIMATE)

Zomba	2946 Ft	Fort Johnston	1700 Ft	Luchenze	2500 Ft
Blantyre	3500 Ft	Dedza	4500 Ft	Kota Kota	1800 Ft
Limbe	4000 Ft	Ncheu	3500 Ft	Chikwawa	127 Ft

Reluctant to contemplate a lifetime of such work without having seen something of the world outside Europe I decided to join the Colonial Medical Service.

Jan Morris, in her brilliant trilogy of the rise and decline of the British Empire[1] describes the system of selection of candidates for the Colonial Service and the man who selected them. Major (later Sir) Ralph Furse, the Old Etonian Private Secretary to the Colonial Secretary, did more than anyone to influence, for 38 years, the type of man selected: all-round men from public schools, University men from Oxford and Cambridge with third-class degrees and good at games. They came to be known as Furse's men, or Furseans. Morris writes: 'They were Sanders of the River, they were Great White Carstairs . . .' and it so happened that it was shortly after watching the film of Sanders of the River in 1935 that I decided to apply for the Colonial Service, tempted by the prospect of an open air, adventurous life, so different from the panel practice in the Midlands. With my adequate but not startling degrees and having rowed, but only for the Caius College 1st May Boat, not the University, I was a typical Fursean.

After taking a six-months' course at the London School of Tropical Medicine and Hygiene and obtaining the Diploma, (D.T.M. & H.), I was posted to the Protectorate of Nyasaland (now Malawi), and was instructed to sail in the Union Castle boat, RMS *Grantully Castle,* in July 1936, for the port of Beira in Portuguese East Africa, (Mozambique) and on by the train which ran twice weekly through that territory to Nyasaland.

THE LATEST AND BEST

TROPICAL CLOTHING, KIT, EQUIPMENT

AND EVERY REQUISITE FOR

NYASALAND

AND ALL PARTS OF TROPICAL AFRICA

can be obtained at

MOST REASONABLE PRICES

from

THE TROPICAL OUTFITTERS,

WAY & EVERITT PENN LTD.,

14/15 PANTON ST., HAYMARKET, LONDON, S.W.1.

Call or write for our latest Catalogues of Tropical Clothing and Equipment.

We also provide highest quality Provisions of every kind, specially prepared for Tropical use.

Every article of Outfit and Kit can be inspected in our showrooms.

WHEN HOME ON LEAVE

Call and select the Hosiery and Clothing you require for Home Wear. We stock everything in Men's Wear of the right kind at surprisingly Moderate Prices.

Our "Service for those who serve Abroad" means that you get without fuss or bother the experienced personal service you expect. A service that saves you Time, Trouble and Expense, by always providing

THE RIGHT KIT AT THE RIGHT PRICE.

Tussore Jacket and Trousers . .	**25/-, 42/-**
Cream Gabardine Jacket and Trousers	**30/-, 42/-**
White Drill Jackets and Trousers .	**21/-, 29/6**
Khaki ,, ,, ,, ,, .	**21/-, 26/6**
Palm Beach ,, ,, ,, .	**39/6, 50/-**
Wool Solaro ,, ,, ,, . .	**85/-**
Cream Gabardine Trousers . .	**12/6, 27/6**
White or Khaki Drill Trousers . .	**10/6**
Bush Shirts	**8/11**
Drill Shorts	**6/6**
Bush Smock	**16/6**
Under Drill Shorts	**6/6**
Spine Pads	**1/11**
Calvin Cord Riding Breeches . . .	**21/-**
White Drill Dinner Jackets . . .	**18/6**
,, ,, Mess ,, . . .	**16/6**
Tropical Weatherproofs	**84/-**
Waterproof, guaranteed all climates . .	**49/6**
Airtight Cases	**48/9, 52/6, 67/6**
Cork and Rubber Helmets, Gents' .	**16/6, 18/6**
Pith Helmets, Gents' . . .	**16/6, 18/6**
Wolsey Helmet	**16/6, 25/-**
Colonial Felts, all Fur	**21/-**
Double Terai ,, ,, ...	**32/6**
Waterproof Helmet Covers . . .	**5/6**
Panama Hats	**7/6, 12/6**
Mosquito Boots, White Canvas . .	**19/6**
Mosquito Boots, best quality Black Glacé	**27/6**
Mosquito Boots, best quality Brown Sheepskin	**27/6**
Airtight Boxes, Wardrobe Trunks, Cabin Trunks, Mosquito Nets, Camp Equipment.	
Ladies' Mosquito Boots . .	**18/11, 25/-, 42/-**
Helmets, Ladies', Cork and Pith . .	**18/6**
Ladies' Tropical Raincoats . .	**75/-, 95/-**
Ladies' Tussore Dustcoats . . .	**35/-**
Ladies' Riding Breeches, Mosquito Boots, Helmets and Sunshades a speciality.	
Children's Pith Helmets	**12/6**
Correct Sun Glasses	**8/9**

Advertisements in 'The Nyasaland Handbook' 1932

In later pages it will be seen how I got on, as, imbued both with my mother's idealism and my father's hard-headed practicality (and a good deal of undergraduate naiveté, even at the age of 27!) I set sail for Nyasaland in the company of six riotous ex-undergraduates, destined to begin their careers as cadets in the Colonial Administrative Service. The voyage was long but life was not all play. Under the benevolent tuition of one of the cadets, I spent the mornings learning the rudiments of the language of *Chinyanja* from the Reverend Alexander Hetherwick's 'Manual of *Chinyanja'*. It was time well spent. The evenings were less so and when I remarked to my cabin steward that it seemed rather a dull ship: 'Good Lord, sir,' he exclaimed, 'I've been on ships where there was one of you and sometimes even two of you, but I've never had seven of you all at the same time!' He had to endure us for seven weeks as the *Grantully Castle,* affected with propeller trouble crawled round the Cape of Good Hope and north to Beira. Some of us were bound for Northern Rhodesia (now Zambia) and others for the Nyasaland Protectorate, both territories little aware of their impending fate!

Notes and References

(1) Morris James (Jan), Farewell the Trumpets, An Imperial Retreat. Penguin Books 1979 pp. 308-311.

Chapter 1

The whereabouts of many parts of our Empire were unknown to the man in the street and Nyasaland was no exception. Some of my friends thought it was in South Africa, but most had never heard of it, and when its situation was revealed, exclaimed 'Oh, *Darkest* Africa!' and made jokes about Dr Livingstone, not being much the wiser or bothering to enquire if it was north or south of the equator.

I had, myself, to find out the details of my posting and discovered that it was south of the equator, a narrow, land-locked strip of the Rift Valley, that great volcanic cleft which runs down east and central Africa. The greater part of it was taken up by the third largest lake in Africa, with the Shiré River flowing out of it to join the Zambezi River to the south. Most of the country consisted of high plateaux, the mountains descending precipitously to the Lake in the north, and elephant, lions, leopards, many species of buck and other forms of game were said still to roam the wilder parts.

Portuguese Mozambique surrounded the east and south of Nyasaland, to the north-west lay Northern Rhodesia and to the north-east, Tanganyika a former Germany colony and now Tanzania. The only outlet to the sea by rail was through Portuguese territory to the port of Beira; from there the railway extended to Southern Rhodesia (now Zimbabwe) and on to South Africa. It was a six-day journey from Nyasaland to Capetown by rail but Government servants were sent by sea from Tilbury, at the Port of London docks, to Beira. The journey normally took five to six weeks, depending on the age of the boat, and they brought out with them all tropical clothes and equipment to set up house for a tour lasting from 2½ — 3 years. A house and basic furniture was provided by Government.

From the geography I turned to the history of Nyasaland. This, I found, was less definite since there were no written records until Europeans arrived on the scene, less than 100 years before. Successive waves of negroes had swept down from the north to Nyasaland over the centuries, and until the Portuguese discovered gold and silver in the Zambezi region in the sixteenth century, it had remained isolated, the Portuguese mainly colonizing the coast of Mozambique, but not penetrating far inland.

In the nineteenth century there were changes in the African population. Part of a Zulu tribe, rebelling against Chaka, their chief, moved northwards from south of the Zambezi. Some of them settled in north and central Nyasaland, calling themselves Angoni, and a Yao tribe came in from the east and settled in the south of the country. During both these migrations there was much fighting and bloodshed to overcome indigenous Anyanja tribes, and both migrating tribes became slave traders in conjunction with the Arabs on the coast.

The arrival of Livingstone in 1849 was the beginning of the fight against this revolting trade by the European missionaries and pioneers, during which they sustained many casualties, mostly from disease, in the next thirty years. Finally in 1889, after a brush with the Portuguese, the Shiré highlands in the south of the country were declared a British Protectorate, (the whole territory later being named British Central Africa, and, in 1907, Nyasaland). Fighting against the Yaos and with the slave raiders in the north continued until 1897 when the slave trade was finally stamped out, the country pacified and a start made with its development. The Protectorate, however, remained poor since it had no direct outlet to the sea for its products (mainly tea and tobacco), and though a railway was finally built through Portuguese territory to Beira, the Trans-Zambezi bridge being completed in 1935, this placed a huge burden of debt on the country. When I arrived in 1936 the

Protectorate was also suffering from the world-wide slump in prices following the Wall Street crash in America of 1929.

The Bantu were sometimes said, then, to be at an Iron Age level of civilisation and I studied the crowd on the platform as the train drew into Port Herald (now Nsanje) station, on the border between Portuguese East Africa and Nyasaland. Expressed in terms of their Age these were not in the least like Iron Age men nor had they any of the plumed picturesqueness of Angoni Warriors or of Chaka's Zulus. Rather they seemed to belong to the 'Trouser Age' with sun glasses, and crumpled worn European clothes. They seemed a somewhat tawdry crowd with their cheap battered suitcases and other gewgaws, but it was unfair thus to criticize them. No one looks his best after a night spent in the cheaper parts of a train. The only really smart African on the platform was the uniformed, tarbooshed, *'nsikari'* (policeman), who strode up and down the platform to prevent disorder (where none was to be seen) and saluting myself and my young cadet companions. These well knew from their Officer Training Corps days that salutes were not routinely exchanged between uniformed and ununiformed men and so were not sure how they should respond, particularly after the first half dozen times!

The sun was not yet up and we were soon aboard the train again and leaving behind us Port Herald with its dank, warm atmosphere like a greenhouse on a dull English summer day. On our way between mountains streaked by falling streams *en route* to the railhead at Limbe we were subjected to the passport and other formalities which were necessary for our official admission into the Protectorate. Thereafter the cadets and I parted, in most cases only to meet again after a gap of years, they being mostly assigned to census work in the bush villages.[(1)] For myself I went on to the capital, Zomba, where I was hospitably received by the Assistant Director of Medical Services, the Director himself being away at the time.

Zomba was the seat of Government and officials' houses, hidden among the trees, were scattered on the lower slopes of Zomba mountain, the more senior officers inhabiting the higher layers. From these houses, some of whose gardens were well watered by irrigation channels diverted from a mountain stream, the view extended over a plain to the great Mlanje mountain, lesser hills arising pyramidally between this immense plateau and Zomba mountain. The plateau of Zomba mountain rejoiced in a cooler climate and more luxuriant vegetation than the town, and, on a lower 'shelf', reached by a rough road, were two or three bungalows used by officials and their wives during the hot weather. Overall was the brilliant blue of the tropic sky.

The African Hospital to which I was posted, as second in command (of two), was built on the plain at the foot of Zomba mountain, and the doctors and nursing sisters working there were housed next to it; the European Hospital was higher up the mountain above the Secretariat. The Director of Medical Services had his office in the Medical Headquarters, a separate building from the Secretariat, where he ruled over the lives of his Medical Officers, Nursing Sisters, Indian Sub-Assistant Surgeons and the African staff, consisting of Hospital Assistants, Dressers, Dispensers, Sanitary Inspectors and Vaccinators. There were also a European Pathologist and an Entomologist in Government service.

The European population of Nyasaland when I arrived numbered just over eighteen hundred people. The doctor in charge of Zomba European Hospital spent about 75% of his time on the medical care of the official European population in the Zomba district, and the doctors at Cholo (now Thyolo) and Mlanje (now Mulanje) in the south, and Lilongwe in the north, were also tied largely to European needs. One medical officer was wholly employed in the medical care of European and

Asiatic officials and non-officials in Limbe and Blantyre, the commercial centres of the Protectorate. Allowing for one-fifth of the European medical staff being away on leave, there were never more than 9-12 Medical Officers on duty in the whole country.

The Africans numbered 1,599,888 in the 1931 census, though some were residing elsewhere at the time. Seven years later a Report by the newly appointed Director of Medical Services, Dr H. S. de Boer,[(2)] stated that for actual district work amongst Africans, in a country measuring approximately 37,890 square miles, (or about ⅓ of the area of the British Isles), only 6-9 Medical Officers could provide full time services. On the other hand, the country 'for ordinary administration is divided into 20 districts with 19 District Commissioners not to mention Provincial Commissioners, Assistant District Commissioners and Cadets.' The situation became worse during the war, for several of his staff were posted to the North African front.

The Medical Officers, I soon discovered, had no adequate clerical staff so that they had to supervise or keep ledgers and petty cash accounts, records and returns and to deal with correspondence themselves, as well as issuing, and being responsible for, medical stores and equipment. Besides this they were responsible for the dispensaries in their districts, run by African dressers, which provided out-patient treatment of a simple kind. There were over 90 of these in the country, from two to seven being provided in each administrative district.

One of the weaknesses of the Medical Service (and of the Administrative Service too) was the brief period that any officer could count on having charge of one district. I was about 2½ months at the Zomba African Hospital, being initiated into my new and absorbing life, and was then posted to Mlanje for seven months, from October 1936 to May 1937, returning to Zomba until October, with an interval of two months in Blantyre — all this during my first two years in the country.

Zomba African Hospital was staffed by a European surgeon specialist as well as a medical officer and was the main teaching hospital of the Protectorate, though much of the teaching was done by the Missions, the Blantyre Scotch Mission having an especially high standard. At the back of the European houses lying beyond the site of the hospital were also the quarters of the African houseboys who were on the European staff, plus a proportion of the houseboys' relations, who for brief periods eluded the vigilance of Zomba Municipal or local staff. There were also Africans who, as was customary, came from afar to enquire after the health of patients in hospital. As a result the doctors and nursing sisters inhabited a sort of enclave abutting into a fairly crowded part of transient Africa of several hundred souls, and at that time their houses were not mosquito — or fly — proofed.

The hazard to European children became apparent to me in my first month, for one morning I received a 'specimen' from my next-door neighbour, the surgeon, with a laconic note: 'I do *not* like the look of this.' And nor indeed did I, for 'this' was a very diarrhoeal stool from his only child, and there followed for me, and him, and the doctor in charge of the Government laboratory who did yeoman service, days of anxious work ending with the child's death from dysentery, the organism responsible being a pure culture of *Bacillus Flexneri.* In those days the sulpha drugs which might have made short work of his complaint, had not yet become available and we treated him with salines and a very light, liquid diet. The Roman Catholic fathers who lived nearby did what they could to heal the Catholic mother's grief at this, the second occasion on which she had lost an only child, (the first from cerebral malaria), but she and her husband were sent on leave shortly afterwards and then transferred to Zanzibar, where at least the medical resources were more effective than they were then in Nyasaland, for it a was richer colony. They had yet another, only, child and I heard that at the least sign of diarrhoea the parents used to be afflicted with an all too-understandable panic. One of my earliest recollections of the beautiful plain, with its little pyramidal hills rising out of the mist and the mass of Zomba mountain behind, is of walking in the cool of the very early morning waiting for my young patient to wake, not wishing to cause unnecessary alarm by breaking into his slumbers. The cloudless sky seemed to mock at my concern.

In a letter to my future wife I mentioned the crowded African population surrounding our houses and a further letter described the process of mosquito and fly-proofing them; and thus the stable door was locked.

To most people in the United Kingdom, the word hospital conjures up a high building filled with orderly rows of beds, and in outpatient clinics, rows of orderly patients waiting apathetically to see the appropriate specialist.

The African hospitals in Nyasaland were very different. Like the European houses they were single storey buildings, built of brick with corrugated iron roofs and cement floors, laid out round a quadrangle of grass or hard-packed earth. The space beneath the roofs was often, especially on out-stations, occupied by bats and sometimes by fierce, wild bees. The quadrangle was bounded by two men's wards, two women's wards (some 100 beds in all in the larger ones), a Hospital Assistant's room, the dressers' duty room, an African nurses' room, an operating theatre off one of the male wards, the European Medical Officer's room and an out-patients' room. The out-patients gathered in a cheerful crowd outside and on the verandah. I wrote home from Zomba that there were

> 'country natives, *askaris* (King's African Rifles' soldiers), convicts (patients from the prison) with their warders, and policemen, all sitting about laughing and chattering and all leaping to their feet and saluting like mad whenever a European comes near . . .'

On out-stations the crowd was more countrified and included more women, children and babies. Round about there were other smaller buildings, male and female isolation wards, the hospital kitchen, food store, drug store and dispensary.

A problem in every hospital before the days of DDT, which only arrived in Nyasaland during the last years of the war and was, even then, in very short supply, were the bedbugs. They infested the clothing and bedclothes of the patients and lived in the cracks of the hospital walls. We attacked the latter with flame guns and put the bedding out in the sun, but it was a losing battle. The patients' relations came into hospital too, sleeping in their own blankets between the beds and on the verandah. They brought their own food in with them (and, sometimes, their bedbugs), and their food helped to vary the patients' diet; to that extent, and for some of the nursing, we depended upon them. The patients' diet consisted of maize meal, beans and, where available, fish. Leaf vegetables were cooked as side dishes. Where there was a water supply, I and other Medical Officers experimented with trying to grow as many leaf vegetables as possible in order to add variety to the patients' diet, but hospital would have been a worse place without the relations and less used as a result.

The Medical Officers had to take a *Chinyanja* language examination at ordinary level, and though there was no time limit, their increments depended on passing the examination. It was less stringent than that set for the administrative officers who had spent a year studying the language before arriving in the country and who also had to pass a higher examination, but my *Chinyanja* studies on the leisurely passage out to Nyasaland in the *Grantully Castle* gave me a good start. I arrived able to ask very simple questions and, more important, to understand the answers. Thereafter I learnt fairly fast through contact with patients and villagers, and my Head Boy, who used to relate little stories in *Chinyanja* to me after supper.

As the Medical Officer of the African Hospital, to me was allotted the outpatient department, with and largely dependent on, an African Hospital Assistant. My outpatients included an African woman receiving a course of treatment for bilharzia, a parasitic worm which lives in the liver and migrates to the bladder wall, where it penetrates into the bladder and lays its eggs. These eggs are passed out in the urine; if the infected patient urinates or defaecates into a pool or some slow running water, the eggs hatch out into *miracidia.* These swim about until they find an appropriate snail. Later the progeny emerge, swim in the water and ultimately penetrate the skin of men or women bathing there. Despite, or perhaps because of, this complex life history, bilharzia was very prevalent, its spread being favoured by the cleanly habit of the Bantu, who liked to wash themselves but who, perhaps in order to avoid their urine beng identified and used through witchcraft against them, frequently urinated into such pools. A course of injections, *antimony tartrate* or *Fuadin,* was needed to cure the disease which was a considerable source of ill health.

One day in the course of her treatment, my patient came with a temperature of about 100°, but as she had no special symptoms, I decided to take a chance and continue with her course of *antimony tartrate. Antimony tartrate* is liable to exacerbate infections, and the following day she presented herself with an addition to her case-notes: 'T. 100.5° BF'. BF!!! I bristled, the more because with hindsight this was precisely my own opinion of my decision. But anyway, who was this unknown critic? I felt in an untenable position and held my tongue, treating the patient with aspirin. The following morning she came with an addition to her entry: 'T. 99.8°. BF-ve'.'BF-ve' stood for blood film negative and my 'critic' (the Hospital Assistant) had very reasonably decided to check whether there were malarial parasites present. Clearly, among the things which I had to learn was to 'keep my cool' until each situation had declared itself.

The role of Hospital Assistant was an important one in the smooth running of a hospital and I came to have a high regard for the skill of some of the ones I met during my nine years in Nyasaland. I liked them all with the exception of one and him, too, I came to like more by the end of our association. Hospital Assistants were given a formal training by the Missions up to Standard 6; they spoke and could read and write both English and *Chinyanja,* and were literate and numerate to the extent that they were able to administer the dose ordered by the doctor to a patient. One of their functions was to be the link between the doctor and his less clever African staff.

The cleverest of all our Hospital Assistants whom I later met, and the most typical of the up-and-coming educated 'infrastructure', was Dan Ngurube. Trained at the Scottish Mission ('up Lake') he stood head and shoulders above his fellows as a clinician, and on occasion corrected the diagnosis made by (unidentified) white Rhodesian or South African doctors, on men invalided out, who had returned after working in the mines in Southern Rhodesia or South Africa.

Where Dan was the cleverest of the Hospital Assistants, Marko Mpelele (trained by the Universities Mission to Central Africa), was the *best.* With a strong admixture of Arab blood, he was in every sense of the word a gentleman, being remembered with affection by every European Medical Officer who had served on an outstation with him.

Elias Sisya was a successful result of a combined effort by the surgeon specialist at Zomba African Hospital and myself. He was brought to our attention by the European Matron of that hospital as a veteran of the 'old school' among our Zomba dressers. He did his work reliably and well but was continually overtaken and passed by better educated but less dependable young men on their way up among the dressers, entering the rat race of aspirants for the rank of Hospital Assistant. So we resolved to give him special tuition, after hours, on the aspects of medical work which he lacked, 'Will you draw a picture of the bones of the arm?', I said to him when discussing some detail of anatomy and he drew an astonishingly crude picture of little blobs which should have represented *metacarpals* and *phalanges*. From there we talked to him about the disease processes of which he had practical experience through his years of work and this enabled him to understand the principles behind their treatment. He availed himself of this tuition to good purpose, qualified as Hospital Assistant, and proved reliable, hard-working and scrupulously honest.

Hospital life in Nyasaland was full of surprises and soon after my arrival there was another one. Over the hospital lawn I perceived a patient, fleeing at a great pace and hotly but vainly pursued by two African medical dressers (male nurses) in their white uniforms. 'Oh, dear, there goes my prospective patient for operation this afternoon' remarked my companion, the surgical specialist, in terms of regret rather than surprise. That it was not an unusual occurrence was suggested by his comment that though the patient had departed wearing a hospital uniform and this had to be reported to the police, this was purely a formality, as uniforms thus 'going missing' were invariably returned unobtrusively by the relations within a matter of days.

There was a fear of hospitals as, indeed, there was in England even then, but exacerbated in Nyasaland by the explanations that were evolved by the Bantu to explain the, to them, unaccountable activities of Europeans. There were believed to exist (probably quite truly) a network of individuals who ate human flesh. It would be wrong to regard these as cannibals, eating their victims, as hostile tribes might eat those whom they conquered, to satisfy their craving for animal protein; rather, they might be held to be ritual cannibals to whom the consumption of human flesh gave magical power. Could the unaccountable habits of the Europeans be explained by the hypothesis that they craved human flesh for such reasons? Certainly the hypothesis fitted the observable facts with ominous exactness.

Why, when a patient was brought to hospital in a plainly moribund state, should he be subjected to an operation to complete the job? Obviously the doctor's explanation was nonsense: that desperate though the operation be, it was the man's only chance of survival and must therefore be performed. If, during a drinking quarrel a Bantu was seen to be stabbed in the chest by a spear aimed by a fellow drinker, everyone knew why he had died. Why then appoint a white doctor to cut him into smaller pieces allegedly to determine how he had died, when everyone knew both this and who had done it? And again, to state that the practice of holding post-mortems after violent death was in order to present accurate evidence to the judge in Blantyre, was, of course, ridiculous. The Europeans derived their drive and energy from the consumption of potted meat, for which post-mortems and post-operational deaths were essential to supply a sufficiency of corpses! And, as if all this were not enough it occasionally happened that the white man, with all the panoply of authority, descended on some unlucky community and demanded from every member of it, specimens of blood, stools and urine. Everyone knew that the possession of such specimens gave the white men power over their erstwhile possessors! To say that from this information the pattern and prevalence of disease could be discerned, and the medical services planned, just did not hold water!

In Nyasaland and in much of the Bantu race elsewhere, there was an additional factor which contributed to the fear of hospitals — the fear of witchcraft. Disease, I found, was not held to arise from natural causes but was the malign effect of magic on the part of another person, an ill-wisher who acquired the power to do this through the possession of some intimate part of the victims's physical body.

With education and time a rational explanation of these beliefs could no doubt have become accepted, but in the meantime the fear of hospital called for a quite simple solution which, after discussion with the Director of Medical Services, I was able to initiate. If the patients would not go to the hospital, I thought, then the hospital must go to the patients. This involved the doctor (in this case myself) getting out of the hospital and, in effect, 'setting up his plate' in a grass hut erected in some outlying village, accompanied by a small supporting team to provide courses of injections, to perform simple operations, mostly under local anaesthetic and, in general, to meet the most pressing needs of the village population. The demand was almost overwhelming, two or three hundred patients might be seen in the course of a long and hectic morning. When I left at the end of a week, leaving behind a dresser to complete the courses of patients' treatment, there followed in the succeeding weeks a steady trickle of patients helped in or carried to hospital by their relatives and friends and left there for more extensive surgery or more sophisticated treatment as the case might be.

I did not delude myself that any lasting good was done, but the object was attained, the fear of hospital and its doctor was overcome. For me, too, there were gains in the form of a more interesting range of diseases and of a more intimate knowledge of what went on in the bush on either side of the road and in the more remote parts of my district. The tale is told of an English soldier, who, asked to draw a map of his travels, scrawled a line across the length of his paper to represent the road, with, on either side of it, the letters: 'MMBA' (Miles and Miles of Bleeding Africa), and anyone who has driven along Africa's seemingly unending earth roads with monotonous bush stretching unchangingly on either side, will feel for our soldier. Perhaps he may have wondered what, if anything, lay hidden in that bush? By virtue of the medical camps, something of the life within the bush became revealed to me and of the intricate, busy lives of its inhabitants, living and working within it. I was able to speak the language by now, not well, but well enough. After a few days in a village everyone knew who I was, and was glad to see me if I strolled in the maize gardens at the end of a day's work, and bore with patience my linguistic shortcomings.

Two of the more unusual case histories will illustrate the interest of the work. At the end of a day a man was brought in, slung in a blanket on a pole, from an outlying village; he was slit the length of his belly to his *symphysis pubis,* a ritualised form of suicide not uncommon among the Bantu, but one which I had not met before.[(3)] His wife that morning had flung at him the ultimate insult that she would sooner sleep with a leper than him and this had been his response. The biting and blood-drinking flies were thick upon his exposed bowels which, parched by the hot sun, were beyond my power to heal. We had six adult doses of morphia left from the week's work and I mixed all these in the barrel of a single syringe and injected them intravenously. The creases of pain which lined his face smoothed magically as they do on a crumpled piece of silver paper which has been thrown on hot coals, and he soon slept. By evening he was still deeply asleep but breathing fairly regularly and, I felt, unlikely to require attention before dawn. I went to bed myself.

At some time in the dark the cock crowed, and I awoke and thought: 'How is my patient?' The next question was how much of the night had gone, for in Nyasaland the cock crows thrice, once about an hour after midnight, then an hour or two later and then a third time, at or just before dawn. Lying in bed in the dark, I thought of Christ's words to Peter: 'Before the cock crows, thrice you will have denied me.' Was this really what Christ said or did he mean 'before the cock crows thrice, you will have denied me'? There have been many different translators of the New Testament and the co-incidence of the word thrice suggests that the reference might have been to conditions as they are in Nyasaland and, indeed, I think the cock crows thrice over much of the tropics and sub-tropics. Occupied with these thoughts I lay waiting for the creatures of the night to call one to another and so reveal the time. Then the partridge *(nkwale)* called and I got up at once and dressed, for when the *nkwale* calls the dawn is always close at hand, and even as I laced my shoes the sky seemed a little lighter. I walked in the dawning light to the tent in which my patient lay. His pulse was still beating and as I felt it he opened his eyes and gazed at me with the calm detachment of the heavily morphinised patient. 'How are you?' I asked. 'I am well', he replied calmly. An hour later he was dead; and the work of the medical camp went on as usual.

Let me now describe one of the rarest of conditions, one which a doctor sees once in a lifetime if at all and which I saw but once, that of extra-uterine pregnancy going to term. An *ovum* becomes fertilised and implanted, not within the womb, as it would normally be, but on the side of the abdominal cavity or on the peritoneal surface of the intestine or of some other abdominal organ. There it either manages to establish itself or not, most frequently probably the latter. If established, it grows more or less normally there, as though it were within the *uterus* and forms a *placenta* whereby the *foetus* draws its blood and nutrients from its mother. (Where the *foetus* has been implanted and fertilised within the *uterus* as it normally is, this *placenta* reaches a considerable size and a great deal of blood passes through the infant's circulation.) The infant's birth is signalised by forcible contractions of the muscle of the *uterus* which forces the body of the unborn child through the bony funnel of the pelvis and out (amidst prodigious stretching of the tissues) through the opening between the mother's thighs. The muscle of the womb then contracts usually forcing the *placenta* (afterbirth) off its implantation site and, by this contracting, reduces the site from which the mother's blood would otherwise continue to flow. Through this marvellous mechanism childbirth is normally associated with a minimum of blood loss and the afterbirth is expelled.

In the rare condition of extra-uterine prgnancy with which we are here concerned, the *placenta* is not implanted on the contracting muscle of the *uterus*. The obstetrician's problem, if he extracts the child, is whether to remove the *placenta* from its site and trust that he can himself control the resultant haemorrhage which may be torrential, requiring substantial transfusions[(4)] or to leave the *placenta* in — a big lump of dead flesh which, in these days, may (or may not) be controlled by the vigorous use of anti-biotics to try to check the growth of bacteria which might otherwise kill the patient. But in the days of which we are speaking there were no anti-biotics or blood transfusions in Nyasaland.

Some years later, I was waiting on the bank of the River Gambia in West Africa, with the leader of the British Empire Leprosy Relief Association (BELRA), and as doctors do, we talked shop.

'Once I had a case of extra-uterine pregnancy going to term', he said.

'So did I.'

'What did you do with the *placenta?*'

'I left it in.'

A look of chagrin passed over his face. 'I took mine out. She died', he said.

'So did mine.'

In the days of which I am writing the patient in that condition had only a slim chance of survival in a hospital, none in the bush.

Many patients in Nyasaland, I discovered, were dissatisfied unless they were given some sort of injection. Among the hundreds of sick, partially sick, and others with backs rheumaticky and aching from the heavy toil of breaking-up the soil with hand tools, enquiry as to what might be wrong with them often elicited, not a direct reply, but the single word: 'Jackson!' Anthropologists of the future may report folk-lore telling of a wondrous healer, one Jack, whose skill was only surpassed by his son's! To spare their disillusion let it be said at once that this word is a relic of the reverence once paid to the dramatic response of *yaws,*[(5)] which used once to be very prevalent, to treatment by arsenicals, which had to be given by injection. 'Jackson' was a corruption of the word 'injection', and an injection was considered to do far more good than any medicine taken by mouth.

Paradoxically, one's very reluctance to impose upon the patient's gullibility had the opposite effect to what was intended. 'The white doctor has a kind of medicine — Jackson — which he is very reluctant to spare', one can imagine the word going round the villages, 'but by stubborn persistence I wore him down. And now I feel a lot better.' In this connection some years later, one of my friends, a Professor of Epidemiology, challenged his students to deny that *placebos* did good, since elaborately controlled experiments had to be designed to discount their action when assessing the effect of some unknown drug. Thus 'Jackson' fulfilled in Africa the role of the bottle of medicine, used to *'purify the blood'* by the panel doctor in the mining district where I had earlier served, and which I have described in the previous chapter.

Notes and References

(1) Census. The census was first held in 1911 and subsequently in 1921, 1926 and 1931. There was no full census in 1936 (in the name of economy) or, because of the war, in 1941.

(2) Dr H. S. de Boer Director of Medical Services, Nyasaland, from 1938-43. From a report 'Medical & Health Services'.

(3) Suicide. I had observed the law by informing the Boma and in due course the District Commissioner and a policeman arrived. I explained that I had taken a statement from the dying man. 'Not', said the DC firmly, 'valid evidence at law'. I admitted that I was aware of this but added that I'd assumed they would want to know how the man had died. Later in conversation with the policeman, I said that the DC did not appear particularly pleased with my information. 'Well', he replied, 'some while ago a prisoner under sentence of death did to himself exactly as your man has done but one of your colleagues had him into hospital and sewed him up and he survived, leaving the DC with some awkward decisions to make. Possibly this has rubbed off to some extent on to you.'

(4) Blood transfusions were a rarity but were occasionally performed under somewhat unsatisfactory conditions without any special equipment. I did one myself successfully on a coloured woman who was aborting at six months. Another to my knowledge was done by a surgeon in Blantyre who, knowing his blood group to be that of a universal donor, thrust the needle into his own vein and collected enough blood to save his ex-sanguinated patient.

(5) Yaws is a specific disease caused by a spirochetal organism, *Treponema pertenue,* characterized by an initial cutaneous lesion, followed by a multiple papular, granulomatous skin eruption, and in some instances by late destructive lesions of the skin and bones. Lesions of the soles of the feet are especially common. Yaws is usually acquired in childhood, but no age is free from the risk of infection.

Chapter 2

Mlanje, where I was posted in October, 1936, was a welcome change from the officialdom of Zomba. It lay in the tea belt at the foot of the great Mlanje plateau, and was my first taste of an outstation, though not as wild a one as I had hoped as the surrounding tea estates, managed by European staff, kept me busy.

One of the peaks of Mlanje mountain which
could be seen in the distance from the MO's house at Mlanje

The day began early in Africa, especially on an outstation. With, or before the dawn, there came the sound of maize (or cassava) being pounded to flour by the women — a musical, muffled beat as the wooden 5-6 ft. pestle descended into the grain in the wooden mortar *(mtondo)*. Sometimes two or three women pounded together or in time, but with a brief space of half seconds separating them. Women worked long hours and pounding grain was one of their first tasks.

Next came the sound of wood being chopped and broken for fire kindling; the kitchen boy's fire to boil water for my tea. The chopping could have been done the night before — but why do today what can be put off to the morrow? Even if it does mean rising sharp at dawn. The tea was brought and the sound of burnt toast being scraped was next heard, for toast was the only thing prepared ahead of time, and roused, I would sip my tea whilst reviewing my plans for the day.

Clothes, daily laundered and beautifully ironed with an iron containing hot charcoal, were left by the bed and, in the dining room, the hospital case sheets were laid on the breakfast table. These were of all patients receiving 'M & B', *(or*

Pounding maize

Winnowing maize flour

Sifting maize flour near Matope 1937

Sulphonamides, M & B being the initials of the manufacturers, May & Baker) or in other words, acute or infected patients whose day's dose might need to be increased or reduced, according to their state. From this, the day's total was compiled at breakfast to be later counted out for issue, with the additional increases or decreases where later found appropriate, on the morning round. Here the patient had his dose counted out into his hand and was told not to leave hold of it except to put two, or the appropriate number, into his mouth, himself, when told to by a dresser. It was a degrading implication, that the dressers could not be trusted not to change the amount of the prescribed dose, or to substitute some similar but less potent tablet, retaining the surplus M & B for 'private practice', or for their sale on the black market, but conditions seemed to clear up more quickly under this *régime.* Since many patients were men with venereal diseases, it was important to render them non-infectious before they returned to their wives.

I then attended 'Out-patients', in order to pick up the occasional case that might be missed in the routine testing of stools, bloods and urines, though these were essential in bringing to light common endemic infestations. Then paperwork (never long absent in the hospital day) was tackled, and such surgery as was indicated. As a rule one operation was performed in the day, because the surgical apparatus equipment was somewhat limited and there must be an interval for re-sterilisation of instruments used for the first patient which might be needed again for the second — always assuming that there was a second.

By noon or soon after, the operatee was coming round; his first act commonly was to reach down with his hand to make sure he was still in possession of his testicles, and that settled, he might in due course solicit the aid of a dresser, or of a relative if one was attending on him, to help him to the latrine to empty his bowel or bladder, and again to bed. Post-operative chest infections were rare among

Africans, probably because they moved around so much. Another phenomenon that was rare among Europeans but could be disconcerting to those attending the Bantu, unless the theatre staff was expecting it, was that early during the stages of induction, *something* (and what that something was I do not know), some confusing concept, flashed through the patient's brain and he leaped up and had to be restrained, lest he fall off the operating table and injure himself. (When I later married, I invited my wife to watch an operation. She entered the theatre to find apparently no patient but only the dressers, who greeted her politely; all were leaning, on their elbows, over the operating table, except the anaesthetist. The patient was held down, invisible beneath the dressers!)

The afternoon was a time of peace. The morning's outpatients had been given their medicines and had gone and if there were nearby sick Europeans to visit they could now be seen. After tea, the night round. Dusk falls about 6.0 pm and it was convenient to do the round about 5.0 pm, when it was light enough to observe from the patients' mien, who was doing well and who was not. There was no electric supply and by the light of a hurricane lamp, minor, but significant facial alterations in expression might be missed.

The hospital day was done; but a mellow light from a lamp in the District Commissioner's office as I returned home, might sometimes illumine one or two Africans sitting outside, patiently. They knew that when at last he was done with his paperwork, the DC would listen to their story, in their own language, without the assistance of an interpreter who might, or might not, keep to himself what they had to tell. Perhaps they were reporting some bit of sharp practice by some influential man, whom they would prefer not to know what had passed between them and the DC. 'Always look into any anonymous letter you may get', I heard an experienced ADC tell his successor. Where village roofs are of thatch and easily kindled, this advice, which might seem questionable in England, became commonsense. So ended a peaceful and not uninteresting day.

The month, too, had its fluctuations. In the first part of it preparations were made for the mid-month's medical camp; in the last part the scourge of paying labour and making up returns, and at the end of the year the Annual Report to the Director of Medical Services.

Jan Morris, as I have told earlier, wrote of Furseans: 'They were Sanders of the River, they were Great White Carstairs . . .' I was well enough pleased at that stage with my open air life and my role in the cure or prevention of disease, but undoubtedly the clerical work involved was a considerable burden. Mawhila, a very patient and painstaking dresser, was to be seen working away every month at the records of disease treated at the hospital. There were, I recall, over a hundred different diseases, divided into at least four age/sex categories — male and female, adults and in-patients, children of both sexes — I have only made a beginning with this categorisation. Lest we, the officers in the outstations, slackened in our zeal, there also came at intervals a missive beginning: 'Whereas . . . etc. etc. . . ' and ending with words to the effect that: 'You, plus the Public Works Dept. Officer (or some other) at your outstation, will audit the accounts and stores of the Public Works Department, Post Office, and so on, of your station.' Most of these stores were in strict alphabetical order and I felt there was some irony in being told to check the number of coffins held in reserve against emergency, before proceeding to the supplies of detonators and dynamite!

The Post Office imposed a peculiarly tedious check, for the financial assets included stamps and postal orders and quinine tablets, of which for some reason the Post Office held a supply. The Public Works Officer, (whose previous experience as a boiler-maker in Glasgow seemed only a shade less relevant than mine as a curer or preventer of tropical disease) and I, were reduced to the expedient of demanding that the local post master should compile the appropriate return in such a way that it would be acceptable to our putative lords and masters. This he managed to do but I felt that the method was tantamount to making him judge and jury in his own case, and was relieved that the occasion for the check never for me recurred.

Mawhila, mentioned above, said: 'Sometimes they write back saying there should be one less female case with malaria and one more male case with bronchitis (or some such) admitted. And they are *always* right! How they know it we cannot understand!' I felt that I was not equal to instructing him in the art (if it can be so styled) of double entry. In any case, though I was not at all sure whether I knew who was Great White Carstairs, of one thing I felt certain. I wasn't going to be turned into Little White Mawhila.

Life on the outstation usually closed down with the setting sun and the preparation of the bath. As there was no running water, it was carried hot from the kitchen in four-gallon petrol tins and poured into a hip bath, a more or less circular container with room for one's legs when leaning against its back. We preferred such baths to the conventional long baths, they seemed to stay hotter for longer and required less water. In the dry season the water supply on some outstations was limited and in the rainy season one sometimes bathed in a suspension of mud. Nevertheless on transfer later, by then a married man, to the Church of Scotland Mission Hospital, near Blantyre, we found the house contained a long bath (but no taps). A long bath was a status symbol usually only supplied to our superiors in rank. Feeling, in our naiveté, that we had come up in the world, we proudly showed this to a doctor visiting us from wartime England. He gazed at it in bewildered silence, then: 'You poor people . . . you poor people' he said, which effectively dampened our pride!

After baths — sundowners, a glass or two of whisky for the men, topped to near the brim with cold water, and soft drinks for the wives, who rarely drank whisky. This was the time to entertain any guest to whom would be offered '*patsogolos*', (literally: 'befores'), perhaps groundnuts, roast and salted or other savoury scrap to whet the appetite; then supper. I dined, when alone, in pyjamas, dressing gown and mosquito boots, these last a necessary precaution against mosquitoes biting the ankles under the dining table, and guests also came wearing them. After supper, an hour or two to digest, to play the gramophone — I had about 20 '78' records — to read the papers sent out from 'Home', to think over the shop of the day and plan for the morrow. And so to bed about 8.30, to be called again at 6.0 am the following day.

The staff of an outstation hospital consisted of a European Medical Officer, an African Hospital Assistant, whose duties I have already described, an African 'anaesthetist' and sundry African dressers, a Store keeper, and for outside work, a Sanitary Inspector and a labour gang.

In a few outstations, instead of a European MO, there was a resident Asiatic Sub-Assistant Surgeon. In Nyasaland he was awkwardly placed between European and African and yet was more cultured and better educated than the Indian traders who did most of the petty trade with the Africans (and were strongly suspected of cheating them). A lonely man, the victim of the deplorable British exclusiveness.

Under the Hospital Assistant was the 'anaesthetist' who was a dresser acting as such. His minimal qualification was to be able to render the patient unconscious without killing him! (On one occasion in an emergency on a remote outstation the anaesthetic was successfully administered by the untrained, unqualified wife of a medical officer). The 'anaesthetist' did not need to have reached Standard 6 and was trained on the spot by the medical officer. When not anaesthetising he functioned as a dresser.

The dressers did as much of a nurse's duty as they could. They were usually Standard 4 men and could read and write but understood far less than one thought they could, as I early found out by asking them to interpret to a patient, what I had just said in English.

The hours of duty were elastic. A skeleton staff was kept on duty when there was no call for a full staff. The relations did much of the nursing and helped the patients to hobble off to the latrine very early after operations, by European standards in those days. No enemas were given to patients before operation and there was very seldom any need — they were the captains of their bowels and I was much struck by the fact that if, among the outpatients, one was suspected of having intestinal parasites and was told to produce a specimen, within 15 minutes he would reappear with a blob of *faeces* on a banana leaf.[1]

The Storekeeper was responsible for looking after the drugs. One day a man came to me who had heard there was a vacancy for a Storekeeper on my staff and he wished to apply for it. He had the necessary experience in other hospitals and his papers showed it, though the testimonials were non-committal on his performance during his tenure of office, which was mostly rather short in each post. His thinness and the marks of *pellagra*[2] on his skin, plus the non-committal nature of his various testimonials, suggested he was an alcoholic and on being taxed with it he was wholly frank, but, he said, he had given it up now. For some reason I felt that he was a spirit drinker who had reached rock bottom, had realised the pit that lay ahead of him, and was in consequence on his way up now. I therefore gave him a job and over the next few months he put on weight and gained in health. I never regretted having acted on my hunch, and I heard later that after years of impeccable service he had died trying to salvage drugs in a hospital fire.

In spite of their title, Sanitary Inspectors had little training. Their duties consisted of going round the townships preaching the gospel of the latrine and spraying stagnant pools of water with oil against the malaria-carrying mosquitoes, for during the rainy season water would collect in unlikely places, for at least sufficiently long for mosquitoes to breed.

In my days at Mlanje, a European patient in the tea belt developed malaria and asked me to explain why, since he lived a mile away from the nearest known reservoir of infection, and kept the intervening land free from potential breeding places of mosquitoes. There were a number of canna lilies growing in his garden and these, on examination, showed small amounts of water between their foliage and stems — alleged at our tropical diseases course in London to be potential breeding places for *Anopheles.* I had to admit that I failed to find *larvae* in any of them but the patient, surprised at this unexpected but potential source, stopped their cultivation in his garden, and *post,* if not necessarily *propter, hoc,* remained free from malaria for the rest of my time in Mlanje. The anecdote is given merely as an example of the need to expect the unusual.

The labour gang was usually a gang of ten or twelve uneducated, unskilled Africans who cut the grass round the hospital, in a Forth Bridge sort of way and did any odd job like whitewashing the hospital wards, sweeping, etc. and cultivating the vegetable garden (if there was one) under the eye of the garden boy, and carrying water for it from the nearest stream. They also dug the pit latrines for the hospital and for Boma[3] employees. The latrines were about twelve or more feet deep and were covered by a thatched roof; they had no seat. Those dug in the village for Boma employees were designed to be for family use and, where possible, were allotted each to a family for their exclusive use. They were then kept very clean and free from flies and offence by the use of ash from the domestic fire. Where, as for example in a village with a market, many strangers passed through, their needs were met by public latrines specially built for passers-by. These had their dangers. One such was constructed by my predecessor at an out-station. As, conscientiously (!) I inspected it, the superstructure, eaten by white ants, collapsed and I slowly descended towards this appalling cesspit. Fortunately before my descent became irreversible a large black hand grasped my arm and my Sanitary Inspector hauled me back. Saved from worse than death by an African! It would have made a splendid caption for one of our newspapers.

In European households in the out-stations, 'thunderboxes' and sand were provided, each with its bucket which had to be removed daily by a prisoner, usually a hut-tax defaulter,[4] through a low door in the outside wall. (That task, plus the coarse-ground maize flour *(ngaiwa),* quite different from 'native-pounded' flour *(ufa),* were the two things most disliked about prison life. On the whole the prisoners were a cheerful lot and the warder, walking on duty with a file of them, sometimes gave one of them his gun to carry.) One day, after I was married, my wife came to me, distraught. The 'Silent Service' of the prisoners had indeed been silent and the bucket had been spirited away while she sat upon the thunderbox, with consequences that need no description. Drastic and immediate action was demanded — need I say from whom? But the prisoner on his return with the empty bucket had a quizzical look and I have little doubt that the prison had one more joke to cheer it that evening.

In the remoter parts of the Protectorate the Boma also kept a team of four '*machila* men' for the doctor's use if he had to visit a village some miles away, off the beaten track where a car could not go. A *machila* was a wheeled chair with shafts at each end. One man pulled between the shafts in front, another pushed at the back and the other two ran alongside to take over at intervals. Even in the fiercest heat they would not slack off their running and sang, whooped and turned somersaults as they went. The spectacle called to mind a *posse* of fiends conveying their passenger to hell. They showed extraordinary powers of endurance and arrived at their destination up to eight or ten miles away quite fit and well able to quip along the way with any villagers they might encounter. These replied in kind: 'You may be all very well between the shafts of the *bwana's machila* but I don't want you between my thighs' was the spirited rejection of a *machilaman* by a dusky maiden whom he had propositioned in passing; overheard, this was retailed with glee by our District Commissioner.

The bulk of the day's work consisted in treating malaria, various kinds of worms, bilharzia, syphilis, gonorrhea and conjunctivitis. A proportion of out-patients had European types of disease — bronchitis, influenza, stiff back due to heavy digging with an African hoe around planting time. There were also a mass of injuries of various kinds — minor spear wounds from quarrelling, wild animal wounds and injuries caused by agricultural activities. Venereal disease came second to chest complaints. Women did not suffer from unduly frequent pregnancies as they suckled their babies for up to two years, but complications due to the misconduct of labour in the villages at the hands of elderly crones were common. The children suffered from diarrhoea and vomiting, malaria, chest complaints, conjunctivitis and children's infectious diseases, tropical ulcers, septic abrasions and scratches.

The medicines available seem, by today's standards, pitifully inadequate. Sulphonamides were with us but not penicillin, which only arrived in Nyasaland at the end of the war and then only in very small quantities. (It arrived too late to save the life of one of our medical officers who died from septicemia, contracted after doing a *post mortem* in 1944). *'Prontosil'* was the first antibiotic available, it turned the urine red. We used *morphine* and various milder pain relievers; *antimony tartrate* and *Fuadin* (by intra-muscular injection) for bilharzia; arsenicals for syphilis and yaws. Heavy metals were prescribed for syphilis, in the form of *sodium bismuth tartrate* which could be very painful. To a patient who complained, I said unfeelingly he would have been wiser to have thought of that when he was making love with the woman. The idea of these serious thoughts occurring to him whilst in *flagrante delicto* caused uncontrolled mirth among the sufferer's fellow patients.

Fifty years ago there were far too few African midwives and I never had one for village work. Women in labour were dependent on the care of old women, who had little knowledge but more experience, including that of a personal nature, and many taboos. Their rationale was difficult to understand; it seemed that where they could go wrong they invariably did so. Women were forbidden to pass urine once labour pains had begun or to open their bowels or to take food or drink. From the earliest pains they were adjured to strain down and a medical colleague told me that he had encountered one patient suffering from thirst, and exhausted by so much straining down that she had *oedema* of the *vulva* and on examination she was found not to be in labour at all.

Any hitch in the process of delivery was interpreted as evidence that the woman had committed adultery during the pregnancy and it could occur that, where the obstruction was protracted, due to such things as malposition of the child, the old women would stand around her imploring her to name the man with whom she had committed adultery. A Marist priest who had much experience of life in the villages told me that it sometimes happened that she named some man in desperation and that after that she did manage to give birth. (It must have been a nasty shock for a man returning from a hard day's work and perhaps expecting to be greeted by the *Nyanja* equivalent of 'Did you have a nice day at the office, dear?', to be confronted by what was held to be proof positive of his adultery!) More often, however, the results could be horrific. Let those of you who have borne children imagine going through four days of strong pains, with neither food nor water (for it seemed to take the old women four days to admit that they had made a mess of the labour). My policy, such as it was, was to deliver the child as quickly as I could and to read the old women a homily on the merits of coming to hospital earlier. Even then one had to be careful to avoid inflaming their superstitions. My routine homily included instructions that they should dispose of the afterbirth privately and in some place known only to themselves, so that they should be unable to bring allegations of witchcraft against me.

As a rule after four days the child was dead and decomposing. The frightful stench which accompanied the delivery of its rotten body, with the patient's rectum sometimes sloughed, is something which everyone of my colleagues vividly remembered when he spoke of such labours. When I assured one woman that under anaesthetic she would sleep and the child be removed, she replied in a hopeless tone, too polite even in her exhaustion to express disbelief: 'Perhaps, *Bwana.*'

On one occasion four wild-looking spearmen bore my patient to hospital. Behind them trailed a group of the old women who for four days had mishandled her. Nevertheless theirs was not quite the usual story. After two days of strong pains she had had one very severe pain indeed and nothing further. Nevertheless the child remained unborn. This is the classic history of a ruptured *uterus* and the child's dead body could be felt lying in the belly behind the muscles of the abdomen. I addressed the old women: 'The child is dead and I fear the mother will die.' 'Yes, yes' they said. 'I shall have to cut in order to take out the child but it will be put in your hands to bury privately (etc. etc.)'. 'Yes, yes' they said again. 'And you will take her home to die in your own village.' 'Yes, yes' they said again. 'Why are they so unusually cooperative?' I asked my interpreter, one of the hospital staff. 'Well', he said, with the usual tone of lofty superiority, 'these are *Anguru,* an ignorant and superstitious people, and they believe that if a woman dies undelivered, she remains so in the other world. This *can* be rectified by their witchdoctors, but the ceremony to achieve this is *very* expensive and you are offering to do it free.' In due course the woman was anaesthetized on the operating table. I opened her abdomen in the midst of a cascade of blood and fluid from the ruptured uterus and removed the child, and the woman stopped breathing. Her pulse could just be felt, however, and I closed her abdomen with three quick through-and-through stitches, (a through-and-through stitch is one which goes through all layers of both sides of the wound, the object being to close the patient up as quickly as possible) and she began to breathe again. What followed was brutal but had to be done if the rumour was not to gain ground: 'We took her to hospital and she died there'. I called and the wild spearmen entered the operating theatre and carried her in a blanket suspended on a pole, still under the anaesthetic, down the slope and away from the hospital. As I watched they broke into a mournful threnody and I thought if Hippocrates could see me now he would turn in his grave.

About a fortnight later, passing through the crowd of out-patients to begin my day I noticed one of the spearmen; in the gaily clad throng he stood out like a cockroach among butterflies. I asked him what he had come for, he replied simply: *'Chingwe'*. *Chingwe* (string) is a collective noun that embraces anything from light ropes to through-and-through stitches such as I had used, and I learnt to my surprise that the patient was still alive and now wanted to know what to do to have the stitches out. I told the spearman she must be brought to me to remove them. He returned the next day: 'No' he said, 'she says she has been in hospital and has come out alive and she does not wish to risk a second visit.' Something in her twisted logic appealed to me and so the spearman was shown how to sharpen the tip and edge of his spear until it was razor sharp and to sever the stitches so that they could be removed.

Hippocrates, mentioned above, said: 'no man could foretell the outcome of a blow on the head or a discharge from the ear.' One day I was in memory carried back to the hospital in Bury St. Edmunds, Suffolk, in which I worked as a house surgeon; it was my first job and I was young and inexperienced (and everyone was kind to me). The quotation was the Matron's firm but gentle way of ensuring that I jumped a little quicker to the fact that an apparently trivial fall was potentially dangerous; I deeply admired that Matron, on whose features was printed the mature nobility that comes from difficult decisions made, and responsibilities shouldered. One afternoon, my 'tin' roof shook and drummed under a tropical rain storm, almost drowning the voice of a planter who had rung to tell me that in carrying his young son, about seven years old, he had tripped and struck the child's head against the stone doorstep. 'But he's perfectly all right,' he went on . . . The rain drummed and I had visions of the streams in spate that crossed the eighteen or so miles of the rough road to the planter's house. 'Hippocrates said . . .' The Matron's voice sternly echoed in my mind. 'I'm coming out,' I said.

The journey was better than I expected, though it was dark before I got there. The streams were still crossable. In the planter's thatched house were he and his wife, the latter a competent looking woman, and their son with a wound on his scalp and a sensible attitude about it that suggested firm though affectionate upbringing. The planter held an Aladdin lamp — which is one with a long glass funnel shielding a wick with a paraffin flame. The boy, without fuss, lay prone on the bed and by the light of the Aladdin I gently cleansed the wound and exposed the underlying bone. Across the line of the cut ran a transverse fracture of the skull. The planter, much interested in proceedings, lent nearer and in so doing set fire to the mosquito net above the bed. His wife instantly thrust her bare arm through the burning hole and extinguished the flame along its edge by a series of clapping movements upon it with both hands. 'There!' she remarked with a pleased smile, 'I always wondered what I'd do in an emergency and now I know!' Much impressed, I asked her whether she was willing to wake me hourly by the clock until daylight, and on her agreement, slept, confident that I would be woken at the stated intervals. At dawn, when the child's pulse rate still showed that there was no intracranial haemorrhage, I ate a welcome breakfast, and drove home without much trouble.

One day word came in from a tea estate that a man from nearby Portuguese territory had developed smallpox and the planter manager was anxious that it should not spread. So, too, was I. I had no fear of a real epidemic; I had in the last month or two gained some idea of the frequency with which the arms of the Bantu bore scars of vaccination. But I had not the same impression of things in Portuguese territory, and the tea estates employed many immigrant labourers who worked for long enough to be able to pay their tax and to satisfy the more pressing of their wants, and then departed. This particular case, if verified, would need to be tightly ringed off lest it spread. 'Damn the man!' I thought. In wrath I planned to make a public exhibition of him, as the fool that could not be bothered to make use of the services of the travelling vaccinators, who, in British territory at least, went from village to village, vaccinating whosoever did not bear recent scars of his or his colleagues' visits.

The estate manager, a pleasant man with a wide knowledge of what went on among Anguru (Anguru are so dubbed because they roll their rs) on his estate, went

Government Vaccinator at work near Mlanje, 1937

with me, accompanied by the Chief's messenger, to where the case was said to be. It was smallpox all right, or to be precise, *Alastrim,* a mild but florid form of smallpox — mild at least from the point of view of the unaffected observer, and this old fellow, his face and much else of him covered in pocks, was very sorry for himself indeed. I had not the heart to add to his woes by upbraiding him for his neglect of precautions. Instead the possibilities of spread had to be looked into. In the village two old women were brewing beer in a tightly — indeed water-tightly — woven basket. The brew would be ready to drink in a day or two and anything up to one hundred men would assemble to drink and dance the night through — and then depart, bearing, some of them, the seeds of *Alastrim* to their various villages. 'This,' I said to the old women, 'is against African law and custom and I shall spill your beer into the ground.' After consultation with the estate manager I paid the old women an appropriate compensation ('though you don't deserve a penny of it!') and spilled the contents of the basket onto the earthern floor. Any thanks that the women might have expressed on receiving the compensation was interrupted by a noise like the lapping of a giant dog. The Chief's messenger, unable to endure the sight of such waste, was on his hands and knees guzzling the beer as quickly as he could. How much he managed to imbibe before the admixture of earth rendered the beer undrinkable I could not judge, but his efforts were loud and lasted long. We departed, planter, Chief's messenger and I, along with a guide for the first part of the journey, in single file with the Chief's messenger walking rather slowly and in due course dropping out. I worried lest he had contracted some disorder from his unusual beverage, and was relieved when he rejoined our file, apparently none the worse.

The following day I received a message from the planter to say that the messenger, when he dropped out of our party, had run back, extracted the compensation money from the women, and in due course had rejoined us. I wrote an apologetic letter to my District Commissioner and he, after enquiry, fixed the messenger with a fearful glare and said: 'If the money is not on this desk before sunset, very terrible things will happen!' And at sunset there the money was!

When walking along a path — almost any path — through the bush, I frequently noticed high against the skyline, four small knots tied in the very tall grass ('elephant' grass[(5)]). Archie Forbes, a very experienced agricultural officer and a fluent *Chinyanja* speaker, and I, both resolved to find out the significance of these, but we invariably received the explanation: 'that is where two people have been fighting, and it is dangerous to tread there.' It was obviously a standard reply for European consumption.

One day Archie came to me in a state of pleased satisfaction. He had been walking past just such a place in the sole company of an African — let us call him John — and asked him the reason for the knots, saying that James, another African, alleged that it was a place where people had been fighting. Now John, as Archie well knew, *loathed* James and his detestation burst forth, the more for the absence of hearers save Archie: 'James is a fool. That is where people have been committing adultery, and if people tread there, there is a danger of *ndaka.'*

Now *ndaka* is a disease in which you become pale, tired, even breathless, and your ankles swell; characteristically, the later stages of hookworm disease. Hookworm disease is due to infestations with a small intestinal worm which causes a moderate drain of blood, and is the prime cause of lassitude in the tropics. Its spread is known to be due to the hatching out of hookworm *larvae* from excreta lying on the ground. The hatched *larvae* generally remain on the surface of the nearby earth and penetrate the skin in the clefts between the toes of those who tread upon the spot. Having thus gained access within the human body (in doing so causing a sensation known as 'ground itch') they migrate ultimately into the intestine, where they lodge, sucking blood. The association of symptoms of *ndaka* with 'ground itch' was evidently clearly enough recognised to lead to the warning tying of the four knots in the grass. The places recognised as being particularly likely to give rise to 'ground itch' are secluded places. It is indicative of the relative importance ascribed to defaecation and adulterous intercourse that the latter, never the former, should be singled out as a cause of *ndaka*.

Sometime later one of my medical camps was in a village which I found riddled with hookworm disease. I assembled the inhabitants for a lecture on its prevention by means of pit latrines. 'Now you people', I began, thinking to strike a novel note in my address, 'suffer greatly from *ndaka,* which you believe arises through stepping on places where people have committed adultery.' At once a ripple of interest ran through the assembly. Here at last was a European who knew what he was talking about. 'Yes, we do.' they said. 'Well,' I said, 'I've been working here for nearly a fortnight, curing all your various diseases, and all I can say is that if your theory about *ndaka* is correct, then there must be an awful lot of adultery in this village.' 'OH, YES!' they chorused, bursting with parochial pride, 'there is indeed.' From then on the lecture followed severely orthodox lines, but I felt that I had lost my audience.

From then on too, I studied with a more informed eye the tiny knots meticulously tied in the grass of the smooth lawns outside the various wards of my hospital.

Notes and References

(1) Dr Trowell published a paper years later on the large amount of roughage consumed by the African, their freedom from constipation and apparent consequent freedom from various other diseases.

(2) Pellagra. A disease caused primarily by nutrient deficiency, which exhibits a characteristic dermatitis on exposed parts. Alcoholics sometimes have some manifestation of pellagra.

(3) Boma. Originally meaning a thorn fence, but later came to be the synonym for the Government, and thus for the District Commissioner's office in each district.

(4) Hut Tax. A flat rate on males over 16 of 6s. Unmarried men were covered by the poll tax, married men by the hut tax. Hut tax was payable on account of any wife in excess of one, whether or not she occupied a separate hut. For taxes not paid before September 30th, the rate was raised to 9s. By special authorisation of the Government payment could be made in instalments or in kind. Penalty for default was imprisonment up to 6 months and forfeiture of hut. Exemptions given to widows and persons prevented from raising tax by age, disease or infirmity. (Hailey 1938. p. 566)

(5) Elephant grass (*Pennisetum purpureum* Schumach.) A grass with reed-like stems, sometimes branching, common in sandy alluvium near streams . . . in uplands only reaching a height of about 2 m . . . widespread at all elevations. ('Useful Plants of Malawi).

Chapter 3

In 1937 I was back in Zomba and held a medical camp in the Zomba district, near the village of Kawinga, a Yao chief whose name crops up in historical accounts of the fight by the British to suppress the slave trade in Central Africa. Kawinga, himself, (for a chief on succession usually took his predecessor's name, and it was automatically conferred on the village where he lived) was a very courteous old gentleman.[(1)] His emissary showed me the sights, which included four little hills rising out of a small plain on which, he said, captives from successful raids were confined by a thorn hedge and watched from vantage points at the top of each hill to prevent their escape. After a week or less, he explained, 'we went into them.' 'Why?' I asked. 'To castrate them.' he replied.

One morning Kawinga asked me for a few cartridges to shoot guinea fowl which were reported from the nearby maize gardens. He departed with three and later returned with three dead birds, of which he gave me one, and very conscientiously returned to me one unspent cartridge, having presumably fired into the flock of birds on the ground, untrammelled by European thoughts of 'sportsmanship'!

A feature of my camp at Kawinga's was the intermittent arrival of patients with lion bites and scratches. It was from all accounts an elderly lion and not very dangerous so long as his prey took the precaution of walking in company, for his companions usually managed to drive the beast off with sticks and spears and such weapons as they had, before the victim was badly hurt, a situation which must have called for considerable courage. If the lion were reported nearby and if the work of the medical camp happened to terminate early that afternoon, I used to cycle out to the spot with my rifle in the hope of seeing him; but the lion had more sense than his pursuer and declined the contest.

One morning a telegram was brought to me by a runner: 'Report to medical headquarters at once.' Hard as I tried, I could not think of any crime I had committed which warranted this urgency — an unfamiliar and uncomfortable sensation. But first I must close down the medical camp, leaving the team of dressers to carry on as best they could. A typical Fursean qualm assailed me; now that I knew there was a lion about was it right to leave my dressers unprotected? I therefore lent my excellent head dresser my shotgun and five cartridges. Then remembering Kawinga's onslaught upon the guinea fowl, I added sternly: 'When I return I shall want to find five cartridges . . . or five lions.' 'Have no fear, Sir, You will find five cartridges.' he replied.

As requested, I reported to headquarters, Zomba, to find that the reason for my recall was so that I might deal with a flare-up of cerebrospinal meningitis (CSM) in the plain that lies between Chiradzulu and Mlanje mountains, through Cholo and on into Portuguese territory. There had been sporadic minor outbreaks (correctly diagnosed) for several months during the previous year, but this was much more serious, with some hundreds of cases. The epidemic threatened the densely populated areas and migratory labour supply of the tea belt, which was in an area of heavy rainfall — about 85 inches per annum.

Before going to the most affected area, I studied diligently such literary material as medical headquarters could supply. CSM, I learnt (and had already known) is a disease characteristically spread by apparently healthy carriers, and in the presence of poor ventilation. Also, (the fruit this, of some observer in the tropics), it abated quickly after the rains had broken. This information was correct. As I drove through the affected villages there were to be observed forlorn looking huts with squares knocked open in their walls by command of the Boma to provide the ventilation for lack of which the disease was presumed to have spread.

Within a month our understanding of the disease and the way in which it spread had radically changed, as had also our method of preventing it. The speed with which it spread, I decided, was a matter of the frequency of intercommunication between villages, presumably because the infectiveness of most carriers was of short duration. It was also obviously related to the numbers of people with whom the carrier came into intimate contact. My early acquaintance, (it does not deserve the title of anthropological study) of witchcraft abruptly rose from academic to one of urgent importance. Death, as I have already written, even death due to obvious infectious disease, is not merely regarded as due to natural causes — true, the man has died of some well-known disease, but who has sent the disease of which he died? To clear themselves of accusations of witchcraft the funeral must be attended by all the relations, indeed by anyone who might have harboured some grudge against the deceased, and a failure to attend is interpreted in the worst possible way by the dead man's relations. As a result men were encountered on their way to funerals of others, dead of CSM, as much as fifty miles away. At the funerals such men would remain for three or more days drinking native beer and inhaling the breath of relations who had already come in close contact with the disease. The visitors then went home either as carriers or to develop the disease in their own villages, and a new focus arose and the disease spread from it all over again.

The mechanism of spread of CSM as a result of social custom appeared all-important. If we could break that custom it should be possible to reduce it from epidemic to endemic or merely sporadic form. One further factor was that the main lines of communication were in the N-S axis, the long axis of Nyasaland, with Portuguese and other territory on either side. A 'clean belt' was therefore created in advance of the spread of the disease, stretching E-W across the Protectorate, where, by vigorous propaganda, people were alerted to the danger of spread by mourning ceremonies, and reminded that these ceremonies used to be postponed, by native custom, in times of smallpox, until the disease was out of the land.

In the establishment of the 'clean belt' I was continually on the move, from village to village by car (if I was lucky enough to scrounge a lift and to be on a road along which a car could travel), sleeping at night in a light tent borne by carriers. I learnt early to walk at the end of my carrier-line, so that the tall grass, its heads soaked in morning dew, would discharge their burden as the carriers' head loads brushed against them, leaving me comparatively dry at the end of the line. Most often I hired some ancient and unsound bicycle. My boys followed me from village to village, catching up with me as I dilated upon the nature of the disease and what must be done by way of isolation of affected persons if, or when, it came, and the waiving of customary ceremonies of mourning, as I have described. My boys had the heavy end of the job, transforming the half-dozen or more carrier loads into a tent, a canvas chair and the appurtenences of a district officer on the move. None of them developed the disease, I am glad to say, and the precious store of sulpha drugs which I kept by me for such emergencies never had to be so used.

I have already said that my earlier toils in medical camps provided an unexpected reward as I was not a stranger to the chiefs or their people. But let it not be supposed that everything went exactly as it should. I called to report progress, such as it was, to one District Commissioner — and to slake my parched throat with an afternoon cup of tea. The DC was out, as his wife, a charming and hospitable woman, informed me, but she invited me to have a cup and I gladly settled into one of the comfortable chairs in her pleasantly furnished sitting room to wait for it; what time she unobtrusively opened all the windows as wide as they would go. Catching sight of my rueful grimace she remarked defensively: 'Yes, I know you — and everybody else — tell me there is no risk of infection, but I have children and I prefer to make sure. As you know, there was a case among the labourers on the station which lay concealed until it came to light. When I spoke about it to my headboy, he said: "Yes, we know this disease means trouble, but we know also that it means trouble with the Boma if it becomes known, and we'd sooner have trouble among ourselves than trouble with the Boma. And so we conceal it."'.

When, later, the back of the epidemic was broken it still left sporadic outbreaks of the disease, and I remembered her story. Assembling a village with one such case arising apparently *de novo* (but in fact no doubt through carrier spread) I explained that there was to be no law, and no quarrel *(nkhondo)* with the Boma. The disease, I said, would impose its own law and create its own *nkhondo* unless they followed carefully my advice. At the close of my talk, to which they had listened with obvious attention, there was a long pause, after which one of them, a young man, asked: 'When can we sleep with our wives?'. It was plain that this native taboo on sexual intercourse during an epidemic, was a key issue between the 'senior citizens', who would insist on applying the old interdictions in times of danger or disaster and the 'junior citizens' who objected to it and could see no good arising out of it. I answered smoothly, 'not for at least a fortnight', to the chagrin of the younger people and to the gratification of their elders. Whether rightly or wrongly I do not know, but it seemed probable to me that the authority of the old would not easily weather such a jolt if I did not uphold them. Anyway, we had no new cases in that village or any other near it.

We waited anxiously for the rains when, if the epidemiologists were right, the frequency of outbreaks should diminish. This diminution did in fact occur, not I felt, because of a change in the atmospheric humidity which had been postulated as the cause, but because with the outbreak of the rains everyone was so busy hoeing, planting and weeding to take advantage of the growing season, that social intercourse was almost nil and so too were the possibilities of spread.

In one respect we overstepped the mark: in view of the apparent role of beer drinks as a vehicle of spread we forbad them. (In times of smallpox their hazard was recognised and they diminished in popularity and size). The immediate effect was that the prisons in the CSM area became emptied or almost so; for stabbings, and fights with spears or blunt instruments are practically non-existent where little or no beer is drunk. But beer has an important social and economic role among the non-Islamic Bantu tribes, and soon the prisons filled again with brewers of illicit beer, or their customers, as the ban was ignored. Indeed the prisons then bulged at the seams and in some areas extra prisons had to be built. However, the epidemic of CSM was rapidly reduced to a minor sporadic or endemic form and the CSM rules became grudgingly tolerated. From east to west small outbreaks occurred along the southern border of the clean belt but the disease never afflicted the main towns or broke through the belt to the northern part of Nyasaland, and more or less petered out in the centre and south of the Protectorate. To my superiors my normally grey eyes assumed a brighter hue of blue, much to the pleasure of my parents, who had come out to see the country for themselves and how their son was getting on.

The containment of the CSM outbreak changed nothing much and even less was changed for the better. Population pressure was all the greater for the survival of five hundred or so of Africans who might otherwise have died. Because of this pressure forest land around the foot of Chiradzulu mountain had to be yielded for agriculture with all that that entailed, but that was another story, as Kipling might have said. True an original approach to the control of infectious disease had been used and with success, but it was doubtful whether the Bantu had learnt much from this and there was little indication that the chiefs, as Native Authorities, were any better organised to deal with outbreaks in future years.

Since there was no reduction in the size of communities, or of traffic between them, the tendencies which had predisposed to the development of epidemics were still unchanged so that it was to be expected that further outbreaks would occur. In fact, such outbreaks did occur in the succeeding years but fortunately they were small. One such occurred near Fort Johnston, (now Mangochi), where I was posted the following year. Breaking out as it did, at the very beginning of the dry season with the prospect of spread throughout the long months before the rains, I stamped it out quickly, but another flare-up was reported from Matope, close to the Murchison Falls, where a bridge was being put over the River Shiré. This presented new problems, as some seven hundred labourers were involved and it was predictable that CSM would occur among them. Of thirty prisoners — hut tax defaulters working on the bridge — no cases occurred during the months of their confinement there. Because the ventilation of their room was unsatisfactory by European standards, there being only one window at the end, the guards were ordered that their prisoners should sleep in pairs, side by side, with each man's feet by his neighbour's head, and vice versa, and this seemed to be sufficient, since no case occurred.

The seven hundred free labourers were less lucky. At this distance in time I have not the figures, but constantly cases would occur here or there among the labour force without any clear reason. Any reduction as occurred was ascribed to evidence (however circumstantial) of reduced contact with carriers and to increased accommodation (in grass huts, hastily built for the purpose). Moreover, the strain of infection was very virulent, and Prontosil, which was all we had to stay its course, did not seem to be much help. One morning I noted a man walking stiffly towards the dispensary and identified the cause by spinal puncture; despite treatment, by evening he was dead.

It seemed that *something* affected the labour force more than the prisoners. Having assembled the labour force I asked: 'Show me what it is you do when you return to your huts to sleep at night.' A good-humoured burst of laughter greeted this, to them, preposterous request, and they all moved slowly off towards their huts, with me following in particular a group of four, all of whom, it seemed, were making for the same hut. Here, in pairs, they wrapped one thin blanket over two of them. Then they took a second such blanket and spread it over both heads to keep off the night biting insects. All was now clear: the fearful fug beneath the blanket was ideal for carrier spread and when they were made to use separate blankets, the outbreak fizzled out.

Such conditions favouring massive respiratory infections from a carrier to an uninfected person might conceivably have been responsible for the virulence of the outbreak, but this remained unproven and largely of academic interest.

When the epidemic in the south was over, I returned to Zomba, but my delight when I was transferred to Fort Johnston in May 1938 was unbounded, for I was glad to leave the gossip and artificial life of Zomba for a true outstation. The Medical Officer's double-storied house at the Fort was built beside the River Shiré. The mosquito-proofed verandah on the second storey looked out on the beautiful prospect of the river, with its islands of *'sudd'*[(2)] floating gently down on the current, palm trees, and hills rising some distance away on the other side. The thousands of bats who dwelt under my roof and emerged in a twittering stream at dusk, helped to keep down the mosquitoes; bird life abounded, hippos squelched through my vegetable garden at night, and a herd of elephant had been seen drinking on the other side of the river the previous year. The Fort was only a few miles from the

MO's house at Fort Johnston, Nyasaland

View from the front verandah of the MO's house,
Fort Johnston

Lake and part of my district could be reached more easily by sailing boat than by car. Crocodiles along the Lakeshore added to the excitement — altogether this, at last, was the Sanders of the River life for which I had joined the Colonial Medical Service.

The European residents consisted of the married District Commissioner, the young, unmarried Assistant District Commissioner, the Medical Officer (myself), an elderly married Agricultural Supervisor, a middle-aged married Public Works Department officer, a young, unmarried English *'Mandala'*(3) storekeeper and a Greek store-keeper, Mr. Phocas. Surrounding the Boma and the scatter of European dwellings were the huts of several thousand Africans and two or three

Asian stores and, at the back of my house, the African hospital of which I was in charge. There was also the Mission Church of St. Andrew, the size of a large room, in which I was married some months later.

The Universities Mission to Central Africa (UMCA), at Mponda's between Fort Johnston and the Lake, housed an Archdeacon and a small Mission staff, both male and female. Hospitable Greek fishermen, the Yianakkis brothers, lived on the Lakeshore, some miles away, and various equally hospitable tobacco planters were scattered on estates among the hills on the other side of the river. These occasionally invaded us for sailing regattas, after which they made merry in the Club. For the Fort boasted a Club house with a bar, a piano, a dart board and a small dusty collection of books. Thursday night was Club night, when the same people, who met fairly frequently during the week, met again to drink, to gossip and to play darts. My wife remarked, in the early days of marriage, that it always seemed to be Thursday.

Besides the fairly staid and respectable officials there dwelt a tiny colony of what we affectionately called 'The Old Soaks', men who had come out to Nyasaland before, or shortly after, the 1914-18 war and had sown their wild oats before settling down to a more placid life at the Fort. A learned graduate, I think of Cambridge, who had come out to study the fishes of Nyasaland pronounced ironically that it seemed that there were two ways of wearing a belt: well above or well below the umbilicus. From which it may be deduced that the umbilicus characteristically lay about a horizontal plane on a belly of considerable dimensions, the fruit of many years of liquid consumption while contemplating reposefully the affairs of mice and men and no doubt other matters of importance. 'Two things, sir, have been the ruination of Nyasaland: the white women and the telephone.' This pronouncement from one of the Old Soaks was unexpected but it was explained to me that a far deeper insight into things could be obtained from the vantage point of the conjugal couch and that white women held forceful views on the colour of skin of the speaker's partner. But the telephone? The trouble with that, he explained, was that it made it too easy for a Director in Zomba to keep tabs upon his flock. And I was told by the colleague from whom I was taking over the hospital: 'When you have been here a few weeks, you will hear the most extraordinary noise coming from this room. It's the telephone.' It happened exactly as he had foretold and it speaks for the remoteness of the outstation that I reacted just as he had predicted.

I had my first encounter with elephants at Fort Johnston. Bob Houston, then a tobacco supervisor, who had scraped a somewhat bare living in Nyasaland for a score or so of years since he had left his native Glasgow, offered to take me in search of elephants near Cape McLear, north of Monkey Bay. We had a licence and wanted to shoot a big one with reasonable tusks. He and I slept near to where elephants had been reported and about dawn enquired whether they had been seen. Yes, said a native of a three-hut hamlet, they had, and they had raided the village grainstores. The little huts, seemingly cowering in the half light beneath tall borassus palms, portrayed vividly the impotence of the African, unarmed against these beasts, and indeed it was common to hear of elephants helping themselves to whatever food they chose, regardless of attempts to drive them away.

With a tracker, we followed directions towards a dense palm thicket which presumably was accepted as the elephants' domain, for the waterbuck and lesser game showed a remarkable tameness, reflecting Man's respect. It was hard to see more than ten or fifteen yards in the thicket, often less, for the water table of the Lake lay only a matter of feet below the surface and shrubs and trees had their roots well into the water.

We were soon in the middle of the herd, a noisy place to be, with branches being torn away for elephant food. Every now and then a young palm would tilt first 15 or 20 degrees, then right over, pushed by a beast's head to make for easier feeding. In the midst of all this din we progressed, speaking in quiet voices, my own from fear mainly. Occasionally a thinning of trees gave a clear view, it was impossible to tell how far, having no object to serve as a gauge. Across one such clearing a line of five or six young elephants moved, too young for our purpose, seemingly in complete silence and calm amidst the noise of their fellows' feeding.

Suddenly the tracker halted abruptly, pointed and whispered 'There!' I peered into a thicket seeing at first very little; then eventually I made out what seemed a quite small elephant's ear gently waving to and fro. 'It doesn't seem a very big elephant to me' I murmured to our guide. 'No, no' he whispered, impatient at my stupidity, 'that's a baby. it's mother's standing just beside it.' Not a glimpse of its mother could be seen! I broke into a considerable perspiration, not ascribable to the heat of the day, and we all softly retreated from the place. Then a chance wind blew our scent to the noisy herd and after one trumpet shriek all became very, very still. The next sound was a tremendous thudding like a giant carthorse running, unhurried, with every footfall separate and distinct. One realised for the first time the point of the honorific Zulu title of 'earthshaker'. It was very hard, amidst the thickness of leaf and shrub to judge how far it was from us, and could only wait for the creature to declare itself. Eventually we had a view of a hindquarter with an

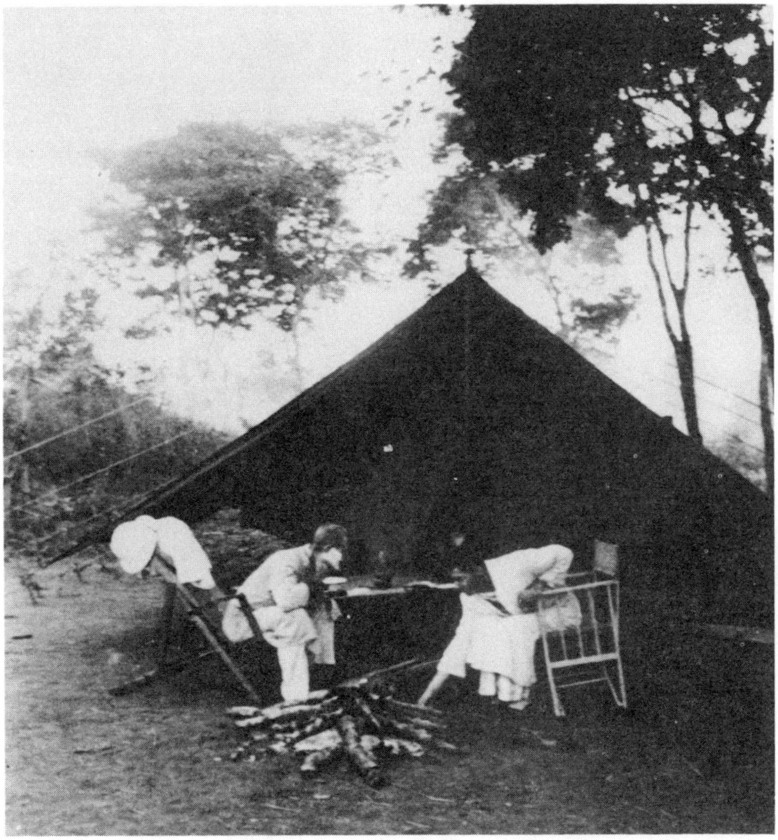

Medical camp near Jalasi's village, July 1939
Shaving on 'ulendo' — W. T. C. Berry & Dr Reg Nicklin

On 'ulendo' — Dr R. Nicklin operating on a patient

Native Authority — Chief Katuli

Chief Katuli's Band

upstuck tail moving across our front. It was a medium bull who, much to my relief, decided that discretion was the better part of valour. I had reached the same decision a significant time before! Chastened, we left the wood.

On that occasion we wanted the tusks; later, as I shall relate, I shot an elephant for its meat among the foothills of the Kota Kota district. The beasts were a continual nuisance in the wilder stretches of Nyasaland, breaking down the bananas, raiding the grain stores and trampling the crops, and any European with a rifle was a popular figure in the villages.[(4)]

Some of my medical camps at Fort Johnston took place in the hills across the river and to reach them my car and all the loads crossed on the ferry[(5)] which was propelled by vigorous pulling on a hawser from bank to bank. The ADC and I found ourselves on this ferry one evening, having descended by car from Jalasi's village, where I was holding a medical camp, near Fort Mangoche in the hills.

Chief Jalasi was the Native Authority, a forceful, beady-eyed leper and a Yao who gave me a lesson in etiquette for addressing him in *Chinyanja,* a slave dialect, but the only one I knew and the official language of Nyasaland. He summoned a bystander and issued a number of instructions to him in *ChiYao,* which was Jalasi's own tongue. This done, and the man having been sent away, Jalasi turned to me and, speaking *Chinyanja* with obvious and exaggerated difficulty, enquired about the progress of my work. As soon as I had spoken a few words in *Chinyanja,* Jalasi stopped me and recalled the man whom he had sent away, who then acted as interpreter in a three-cornered conversation. From this I inferred, as it was intended that I should, that it was not 'done' to even harbour the supposition that a great chief of a conqueror tribe, the Yao, had any comprehension of *Chinyanja,* a language of former slaves. At a later date, and to coincide with *Idi,* a day of great rejoicing among Mohammedans, Jalasi sent three presents to the Boma. The first, a knife about the size used to slash grass in clearance work, was for the District Commissioner. The second, of lesser size, was for the ADC. The third, smaller yet, was for the Medical Officer. The DC, a tactful man, remarked that mine was of far more daily use than his own 'mini sabre', but the message did not need to be underlined!

Once on the ferry, the ADC, a Herculean man, put his great shoulders to the hawser and I put my scrawny ones, and ferry, car and passengers all, a few of whom offered help, shifted at a good pace across the stream. The following day in the hospital, a very agitated man asked me not to tell his uncle Jalasi that he had not helped us at the rope. I reflected that the concept that it was *'infra dig.'* to undertake manual labour did not make for good in Nyasaland and regretted that it might owe its origin largely from the example set by Europeans.

A few days later, sailing in a dinghy past the ferry, I observed it to be at a standstill, while a confused and angry shouting filled the air. I asked my crew what they were shouting. 'They say if he won't pull on the rope, why should I?' I tied up a little way down the river where I could watch without being observed. After a while the shouting died and, pulled, it would seem by a few men who could see that if no one made a move they would never get across at all, the ferry crept 'like snail' across the river. Sadly I reflected on the prospects among these Bantu of co-operative effort. Nevertheless it was noteworthy that in the succeeding weeks the ferry seemed to get across without too much delay or fuss. Possibly they felt the grim eye of Jalasi on them; possibly they had come to accept the inevitability of concerted action.

The regulations then governing the Colonial Medical Service forbad young doctors to marry during their first tour except with the permission of the Director of Medical Services. The youngest sister of a Cambridge friend and I had met fleetingly when she was fourteen and I was twenty, and not again until a month before my departure for Nyasaland, nearly six years later. We then corresponded about once a fortnight and towards the end of the three years of my tour, with war coming ever nearer, I suggested she should come out to Fort Johnston to stay with friends of mine for three months. We would then have an opportunity to get to know one another again and she could become acquainted with the crude conditions of the bush. Our plans for her travel out to Nyasaland by sea were precipitately cancelled when I contracted dysentery and when, on recovery in Zomba Hospital, my home leave was put forward. A few weeks later it was put back again to the month of July, and since war then seemed imminent[(6)] I suggested she should fly out. (This was still so unusual that word went round Nyasaland that Bill Berry was getting a wife out by airmail on approval!)

So, having first obtained permission to leave my district from the Director, I met my unofficial fiancée in April 1939[(7)] at Chileka Airport, worn and wan after a six-day bumpy flight by the recently instituted Imperial Airways flying boat service to South Africa.[(8)] We had been invited to take tea with the Director and his wife in Zomba, no doubt so that she could be 'vetted' and we then drove the further 75 miles to Fort Johnston that evening.

Two days later, all thought of waiting for three months having fled, we decided to get married as soon as the banns and the Director permitted, and the whole of the European population of Fort Johnston took a personal interest in our wedding. The Old Soaks whom she admired (using the word in its derivatory sense: 'lit. wondered at . . .') as wholly unfamiliar — and perhaps not wholly desirable — amazed her by

A

CERTIFICATE OF

CONTEMPORARY TRAVEL

This is to certify that

MISS V.A. HOLME

has flown over the equator in the *Empire* flying-boat the CIRCE

thus becoming one of the progressive band of travellers who cross the line by air. Over the waters of Lake Victoria, the Lingga Archipelago, the *Empire* flying-boats pass in a moment from hemisphere to hemisphere, beyond the zone whose dwellers recognize no alteration in the length of night and day

'Born with the sun they travelled a short way towards the sun,
And left the vivid air signed with their honour'

Stephen Spender

Longitude 34° 15'E

Latitude zero

22-4-1939

[illegible signature] Commander

Certificate issued to each passenger on crossing the Equator in the flying boats of Imperial Airways. 22nd April 1939

Washing-up in the River Shire,
Fort Johnston

producing the most delightful wedding presents, mainly pieces culled from the equipment with which they had come out to Nyasaland much earlier in the century: a Royal Doulton coffee service, a large silver-plated tray (which later she found the kitchen boy scrubbing with sand as he washed-up in the river at the bottom of the garden), for one or two of the Old Soaks were well-connected black sheep.

Fort Johnston was unused to weddings, ours was only the third in the Mission Church Register, and there was much about the way in which the Fort comported itself which was strange to her, but it was very warm and friendly, and ended on a suitably romantic note on May 24th (Empire Day), as I rowed her and my dog across the Shiré after the reception. The wedding was graced by the presence of my Director, Dr de Boer and his wife, the married officials of the Fort, the UMCA Missionaries and thirteen unattached men. The District Commissioner acted as father of the bride and the reception was held at his house.

My fiancée and I had defied the convention that we must not meet before the ceremony, by driving up into the hills that morning to our honeymoon cottage (lent to us by the Government Entomologist who was on leave) and picking a bunch of his roses. This she made into a bouquet with the tinfoil from a tea-box wrapped round the stalks, covered by a satin ribbon from a chocolate box, provided by the District

Empire Day — 24th May, 1939
Archdeacon Wynspear UMCA, W. T. C. & V. A. Berry
Mr. Fromings UMCA, Punch

Commissioner's wife. Her wedding ring had been bought from an Indian store by Commander Farquaharson in Limbe, (he was one of the many drowned when his ship turned turtle in a gale on the Lake in 1946), and my best man was a young layman from the Mission, who stepped in to take the place of one of my ADC friends, smitten with malaria 200 miles away. The Archdeacon of the Mission performed the ceremony.

We had left the car on the opposite bank in the morning, re-crossing the Shiré on the ferry and, after the reception, still in our wedding clothes — in my case a white suit, resurrected from a tin-lined trunk and yellowing at the creases — we stepped into a rowing boat and, as in a film, 'disappeared into the sunset' for three days' honeymoon. There was to be a sailing regatta at the Fort on the fourth day and I was anxious not to miss it!

Outside my house in Fort Johnston a large bougainvillea of unusual colour rioted, watered daily from my bath. My wife, a new broom sweeping clean in a bachelor's abode and horrified at the number of small ants *(nyerere)* which happily swarmed in the damp conditions of the bathroom — merely a room on the second storey with a cement floor and a hole in the corner through which the bath water was emptied — ordered that it be disinfected and scrubbed. I first became aware of this when I returned at the end of a day's work to find the bougainvillea, which was my pride, lying withered and dying from the disinfectant to which it had been subjected. It was the beginning of a new *régime* in my life and indeed, my bachelor friends are said to have observed many changes in me.

My poor wife! Early in our married days I came upon her gazing accusingly at three worried-looking houseboys before the open door of our small paraffin operated refrigerator. 'I think the smell comes from that,' ventured my head boy, pointing to a tightly closed receptacle lodged in the coldest part of the machine. 'That', I fear, contained the stomach from a corpse, suspected of having died from poison, which I had had dug up and on which I had performed a *post-mortem*. I was keeping the stomach and its contents as cold as possible pending its transport by lorry to Zomba for further examination but had forgotten to tell my wife.

My poor houseboys! Soon in our married life three little vertical lines appeared in her brow, which I called 'Ali, Ngondo and the kitchen boy', these being the unfortunates who most signally failed to come up to London standards. Yet by the standards of a bush bachelor they were excellent boys; scrupulously honest, capable of adapting to rough and varying conditions which changed often every day, in the hard travel across the face of Nyasaland during the hasty consolidation of the 'clean belt' that had proved so effective a block against the spread of cerebrospinal fever. Rough boys — certainly you would not expect to find them in the Ritz. But nor would you, in the Ritz, expect to have your first course brought to you by a waiter, quite literally drenched to the skin by a sudden tropical thunderstorm, and announcing with mock solemnity: 'Rain soup!' *(Soupo wa mvula)*. It says much for all concerned that most of my boys stayed with us for years before both sides ultimately came to regard the clash of cultures as incapable of resolution.

At the end of July, 1939, we went on six months' leave and a week after we landed in England, war was declared. In the early months of the war a concept was maintained among the high government circles that this was to be 'an economic war'. My wife, exploring for me in London the possibilities of transferring to the Navy, was told at the Colonial Office that I would be far more use back at my job in Nyasaland than 'rushing about in uniform waving a flag!' And quite soon, on a Saturday, I received a telegram warning me to be ready to report for duty the following Wednesday, ready to sail with light luggage only and without my wife. She, however, suggested that we should immediately enquire at the Crown Agents whether there might be room for her on the boat. The chance seemed remote but we both travelled to London from Tunbridge Wells early on the Monday. To our astonishment we were assured that there would be no difficulty, provided we could produce a doctor's certificate to the effect that she was fit to travel (in effect, that she was not pregnant). This I was able to provide on the spot, but a friend, the Director of Customs, standing next in the queue, was in despair. He lived at Pevensey in Sussex, and could not get a certificate from *his* doctor in time before the boat sailed. Needs must when the devil drives — I wrote out a certificate for him on the only paper available, a routine form supplied at the Crown Agents, (state nature of business, with whom etc. etc.). The clerk behind the desk refused to accept it. I said: 'I am a doctor and this is a doctor's certificate.' The clerk retired to consult with his superiors, on his return he said: 'All right — if you write it on a proper piece of paper!'

At Tilbury, the exit port, everything went smoothly, though we met some of our Colonial colleagues whose 'light' luggage consisted of little more than a suitcase apiece — and no wife. The voyage to Capetown was uneventful. The ship was a fast Union Castle mail steamer and we headed right out into the Atlantic to avoid the German pocket battleship *'Graf Spee'*, which was said to be hunting nearer the coast. We were blacked out at night and carried a small gun which the younger male passengers helped to man during the day, and life-boat drills were frequent and well attended; but life went on much as in peace time, with quoits and deck tennis competitions, dancing and games in the evenings.

We travelled up to Nyasaland by train from Capetown. It took the best part of a week and on arrival, I was asked: 'What on earth have you come back for?' for we had had only six weeks leave instead of six months. It transpired that my name was on a list of men who must come back if war was declared, since it had been assumed that Italy would immediately enter the war against us on the North Kenyan border, where my medical services might be required. In the flurry that followed the outbreak of war, although Italy remained neutral, I was nevertheless recalled, as were my sparsely-luggaged and wifeless friends, and I understand that they unnecessarily spent four years or more in enforced separation, the one in East or Central Africa, the other a grass widow in England.

Not knowing what else to do with us, the Director of Medical Services sent us to Dedza, 5000 feet above sea level, on the Lilongwe-Fort Jameson road, two miles from the Portuguese border, where I replaced the Medical Officer who was then sent on leave!

The headquarters of the White Fathers' Mission was only eleven miles from Dedza and I was consulted one day by one of the Catholic priests because of intense pain arising when even slight pressure was applied to an incisor tooth which had a gold crown. The diagnosis was not difficult and the treatment needed was clear; he had an apical abcess and the tooth must be extracted under general anaesthetic. Dr B. S. Platt, who happened to be there, and who comes into my story later, agreed to give the anaesthetic — open chloroform for want, on an outstation, of more sophisticated means of inducing unconsciousness. By means of paraffin lamps we lit the operating theatre, and all went well until I applied the forceps prior to extraction. Unexpectedly, the gold tooth — or to be precise the gold crown to the tooth, behaved between the jaws of the forceps like a pip squeezed between some schoolboy's fingers. It spurted out and in the dim lamplight could nowhere be seen. From the patient's point of view the effect was wholly satisfactory; the apical abcess was drained, which was the object of the exercise, and when the infected root had settled down it could be removed. The only question was: 'Where was the gold crown?' There could only be two places, outside or inside the patient and a search on the theatre floor revealed nothing nor did a search inside the patient's mouth and pharynx. Being an outstation there were no facilities for X-ray; had there been we could have sought for it in his chest confident that the metal would have shown up on X-ray. In the morning also, a meticulous search revealed nothing in the operatng theatre. We must not risk leaving it in the patient's chest. Petrol tank and radiator therefore filled, and with the bewildered patient, I embarked for Zomba, down the rough road, where soon after mid-day, his chest was screened and yet again nothing was revealed. The radiologist took X-ray photographs of the patient's chest and abdomen against the possibility that the gold tooth had been swallowed; he had not opened his bowels and with the accelerator pressed hard down, we set off on the long trip home. 'I think it is the *Bwana* Doctor driving,' a resident at Ncheu was told by her head-boy, studying the approaching cloud of dust, 'because his car is leaping upon the road.' 126 miles of leaping on the road and I returned the grateful priest to his Mission.

A fortnight later I received an X-ray report: no gold tooth anywhere seen. Where then was it? I have no doubt that one of the African theatre staff had quickly concealed it when it first flew out of the patient's mouth, to sell later. Over 250 miles of hard driving for nothing! I went to the Mission to give him the news but the priests were at their devotions which I did not wish to disturb. Later, I received a letter: 'Doctor, we were at our prayers when you came and we did not hear your silentious motor car!' I wondered (and still do) how much that chap got for the gold tooth?

By Christmas my wife had made the curtains for the Dedza house and we settled down to married life in our new home, but at the end of December I was informed that we were to be transferred to the Kota Kota district, there to take up a special assignment. I must digress in order to explain what it was and how it came about, as it altered the whole course of my life.

Notes and References

(1) Kawinga's predecessor is mentioned in the literature as an active pro-slaver!

(2) Sudd. Floating plants, trees, etc., impeding navigation. (Arabic = barrier. OED)

(3) Mandala. The African Lakes Corporation, Ltd., the pioneers of trading in Nyasaland and Northern Rhodesia (now Zambia), established 1878. The brothers J. W. and F. M. Moir were sent to Nyasaland as joint managers and the headquarters of the Lakes Company were fixed at Mandala outside Blantyre. Mr. J. W. Moir wore spectacles so was called 'Mandala' by the Africans, meaning glass. This nickname was applied to his residence and came to mean both the Company and the place where they settled near Blantyre. In the eighteen nineties the Company operated two paddle steamers between Murchison Cataracts and the Zambezi delta. (British Central Africa)

(4) 'The use of game pits is prohibited by law. Nevertheless pits in use are still occasionally found in the bush . . . The animal caught in the trap is speared to death or, if an elephant, a fire may be lit on its head or a poisoned arrow shot into it . . .' (From a paper 'Traps and Trapping', written by William Rangeley, found among the *Nyasaland Survey* papers.)

(5) The Fort Johnston ferry. The Government bought a 40' stern paddle-steamer, the *'Childeru'*, originally named *'The Swan'*, for use as a ferry at Fort Johnston, from the University Missions to Central Africa in 1922. She had been assembled at Malindi in 1899 and in 1907 was converted to a houseboat for visiting Mission Stations on the Upper Shire, propelled by punting. She was still in service as a ferry in 1937. (I think she was still there when I was at the Fort in 1938/39). ('Lake Malawi Steamers')

(6) The Munich Agreement, a capitulation to Hitler, had taken place in September 1938, and most of us were convinced that war was inevitable.

(7) On Good Friday 1939, Italy seized Albania, a few days before my unofficial fiancée's flight. As a result Brindisi was swarming with Italian troops and no landings by Imperial Airways were allowed although it was an official stop.

(8) Imperial Airways was formed in 1923 from the amalgamation of several companies for the development of Empire Air Routes. In 1931 there was a service to Kisumu which was extended to Capetown in 1932, taking eleven days; in 1934 this was reduced to 10 days and in 1935 to 9 days. In 1937 Imperial Airways discontinued the service to Rand Airport and inaugurated the flying boat service down the east coast to Durban, taking 6½ days. Rhodesia and Nyasaland Airways provided feeder lines. In the summer of 1937 the Empire Air Mail scheme began. (Hailey's African Survey)

Chapter 4

It was in the early nineteen thirties that the Yugoslav delegation at a League of Nations meeting drew attention to world food shortages and proposed that the position in all representative countries should be investigated. In 1935 the Australian delegate brought up the matter again and a Report was subsequently produced entitled *'Nutrition and Public Health'*, which revealed that poor countries were suffering an acute food shortage and, as a result, committees were set up to co-ordinate a World Food Plan.

In 1936 the Secretary of State for the Colonies in the United Kingdom sent a despatch to British Dependencies, asking for comments and recommendations. In Nyasaland a certain amount of work on Nutrition and its relation to agriculture, public health etc. had already been done,[(1)] but the Native Welfare Committee then sent a questionnaire to all District Commissioners, Missions, Agricultural and Forestry Officers, Medical Officers and educated Africans, asking them for certain other details. These included tribes and their staple food crops, cash crops, methods of cooking and differences in feeding, average acreages cultivated per family, soils, deficiency diseases, etc. in each district. On receiving the results, the Committee considered that, in order to raise the standard of living, certain investigations should be carried out,[(2)] and these recommendations were sent to the Secretary of State.

In 1937 a Committee on Nutrition in the Colonial Empire was set up by the British Economic Advisory Council to examine the reports coming in from British Dependencies, and, as a result, Nyasaland was chosen as the venue for a Nutrition survey. The Medical Research Council then appointed a Central Nutrition Research sub-committee to co-ordinate nutrition surveys and research. This was necessary since the International Institute of African Languages and Cultures[(3)] (now the International African Institute), already had under consideration proposals for a Nutrition Survey in one or more East African tribes. The two projects were fused and the Institutes proposed Survey broadened in scope; it was to be the first of a planned series of comprehensive Surveys throughout the Empire.

The following year a Dr B. S. Platt was appointed to head a team of scientists carrying out the Nyasaland Nutrition Survey, which was intended to be in the field for one year.

Dr Platt had had a brilliant career. He trained first as a chemist, but after obtaining a 1st class degree in 1923 at Leeds University, followed by M.Sc. and Ph.D., he switched to medicine, graduating with honours in 1930. From 1932 to 1938 he was an associate in medicine at the division of clinical research of the Henry Lester Institute of Medical Research in Shanghai, where he (with Dr G. D. Lu) discovered the role of B1 (thiamine) in *beri-beri*[(4)]. Having to leave China because of the political situation he returned to England, joined the staff of the Medical Research Council and was then appointed Director of the Nutrition Survey organisation. He had thus spent the first twelve years of his career in England, followed by six years in China, and at the age of 35 was embarking on a new venture in Africa.

Platt was a Yorkshireman, fair-haired, big, deliberate in speech and forceful; he was widely read and had an excellent memory. One of his Survey team, writing home, remarked that he was persistent, and that: 'he is nearly always right when it comes to an argument. It is wiser to give in early on, anyway he *is* usually right about whatever it is.' The Medical Officer appointed to the Survey was able to hold his own only when it came to local customs and language, about which he and the other Government officials seconded had a good knowledge.

Platt had the visionary outlook of the eminent nutritionist Lord Boyd Orr, and having established his vision as desirable and necessary to attain, it was for others to overcome the obstacles that lay between. The success of the visionary lies in his ability to inspire others with the necessary fire, and if he does not his task becomes hard — and Platt often expressed his impatience at the slow and limited minds of Furse's men, and in some cases did not bother to conceal his scorn of the individual. His energy was prodigious and he bubbled with ideas, nothing seemed impossible as later he outlined his schemes to us for a Nutrition development Unit to carry on after the Survey. It would be run with Colonial Development Fund money, with the backing of the Medical Research Council and the Colonial Office, and his influence would bear on those in high places.

I was infected by his enthusiasm and so were others — the younger men; the older ones in Government service took a more detached view, born of their struggles in carrying out the policy of Indirect Rule, introduced into Nyasaland in 1930.

To explain the workings of Indirect Rule and why it was introduced, it is necessary to go back in time to the early years of the century. In a country barely tamed, still only recovering from the traumata of the slave trade and desperately poor, a great deal had been done by the energy of District Commissioners and by their firmness in seeing that what had to be done, *was* indeed done. This was achieved with the good will of the local population — a miracle of diplomacy and tact. But much of it was done almost in spite of, rather than because of, the chiefs, whose authority, damaged by the forced suppression of the slave trade, was in danger of disintegration.

Lord Lugard, noting this in West Africa, introduced the concept there of the Dual Mandate and of Indirect rule, whereby much of the major duties of the State was carried out through the chiefly structure indirectly rather than directly. In 1930 this system was introduced into Nyasaland. This did much to salvage the indigenous authority and much of it was work to which the chiefs were used by custom and still had the power to perform. But with the decades of the Pax Britannica, problems had changed both in nature and in tempo; no longer had the chiefs to rally and organise their peoples against obvious dangers of aggression from outside. Now the problems were within and more insidious: increase in population leading to soil erosion and the slow destruction of natural resources, necessitating adoption of new agricultural methods to replace shifting cultivation — or slash and burn. The Bantu were now living in an environment too subtle for their comprehension and the exercise of chiefly duties all the more difficult to explain, and unpopular because of this.

Few of my fellow Furseans themselves had a good word to say for Indirect Rule, but one point in its favour was brought out later by Dr. Fitzmaurice in the Medical Section of the Nutrition Survey. Since its introduction, Chiefs, as Native Authorities, conducted their own Court Cases so that witnesses and others from the hills did not need to travel down to the Administrative centre of Kota Kota on the Lakeshore, and there was a marked decrease in the malaria patients in the hill village studied in the survey, as a result.

The Chiefs varied enormously in character. I, personally, met three who were outstanding besides Jalasi, mentioned in the previous chapter. They were Kadewere in Chiradzulu, who supported me during the cerebro spinal fever epidemic, Mabuka in Mlanje and Gomani in Ncheu. Gomani was a strong man, as well as intelligent. I had recourse to him when, due to misinformation as to the rate for the job, I met with flat refusal by my carriers to carry my drugs and dressings to a village in the Dedza district where I planned one of the medical camps. This was my first meeting with Gomani and I was struck by the brilliance of his eyes, reminding me of the eyes of elephant hunters whom I had met. I think that the eyes of each shone for the same reason: life to them was exciting and interesting. Gomani listened in silence to the carriers' dissatisfaction. 'Yes', he said eventually, 'the price is bad . . . but it is to help your brothers.' Without a word the carriers took up their loads and set off. I walked with them to the site of the medical camp, to which I had not been before. It was further and harder than it appeared on the map because it involved a steep descent of the escarpment of the Great Rift before debouching onto the plain and I paid the men correspondingly more.

Even so-called bad chiefs had their chiefly moments. I heard that one of them in a village in the Southern Province was sitting gossiping with his cronies when a buffalo entered the village. This apparently was a bull which in his old age had felt an urge to re-visit the haunts of his youth which had become settled as a result of immigration into Nyasaland from Portuguese East Africa. In a flash the chief and his cronies had disappeared from outside the hut where they had been talking; but they were not running *away* from the buffalo, they were running towards it, carrying the hoes which they had been using earlier. At their head was the Chief who smote the buffalo between the eyes and the beast then sank to the ground beneath a rain of blows from the various implements. Here we have an example of a chief literally leading his people, but in a situation more akin to that to which he had been used before the Europeans came.

In her book, *'Lugard: The Years of Authority',* Margery Perham writes: '. . . . At a later stage a good system of administration is liable to a peculiar penalty. Created by men or . . . by a man of high ability, it may become sanctified by its own success and may be reverently or lethargically prolonged by lesser men until it ceases to meet the changing needs of the time . . .' and she adds later:
'it is now easy to see in many parts of Africa that where the vital current of a chief's responsibility running downwards towards his people was diverted into responsibility towards an alien power suddenly imposed above him, the whole character of his office was changed. The change was intensified because at the same time, the chief was expected to use his new and increased power to enforce novel measures. It was as if the institution of chieftainship was a hollow statue, out of which the real traditional content of native power was almost imperceptibly draining away while the white ruler was, equally unostentatiously pouring in his own power in substitution, the outward shell of the institution looking the same while its inner substance was gradually changing.'

Margery Perham thus describes in restrained terms the effect of what came to be spoken of as 'direct rule masked as indirect rule', upon the chiefs or Native Authorities. She does not dilate upon one effect upon the NAs about which our DCs complained: that the chiefs resented bearing an odium, which more rightly should have been borne by the occupying power, of introducing new measures which were not well understood by the Bantu and of which the main purpose was prevention, at this early stage, of the insidious processes I mentioned earlier. By an unenthusiastic attitude they let it appear that their role in practice was to act as a brake between their people and the innovating power. My own view, looking back, is that an element of this was at the back of the DC's complaints about 'useless NAs' and was also an element in our difficulties in getting certain measures adopted when the Nutrition Development Unit was formed after the Nutrition Survey.

The Nyasaland Nutrition Survey was planned on the ideas outlined in *'The Nutritional Review of the Natives of Nyasaland'* submitted to the Secretary of State by the Native Welfare Committee in 1936. The nutrition of a people was to be studied as only one part of a whole survey of their lives and the Review stressed the importance of including an anthropological survey. Since Dr. Margaret Read, a Lecturer in Anthropology at the London School of Economics, had made a study of the Ngoni tribe in the Ncheu district of Nyasaland, the Survey investigations were to be conducted in an area of Angoniland. As a contrast a Lake shore district populated by a different tribe (Achewa) was included, and the Kota Kota district was chosen.

Dr Read was in the team which initially consisted of:

H. G. Fitzmaurice, MRCS, LRCP. (Medical Officer, seconded by the Nyasaland Government).
R. W. Kettlewell, B.Sc., Dip. Agri. (Cantab.) AICTA. (Agricultural Officer seconded by the Nyasaland Government)
M. H. Read, MA., Ph.D. (Anthropologist)
Miss J. Barker, MA. (Nutritional Investigator)
Miss F. Owen, B.Sc. (Botanist, also to act as secretary)
B. S. Platt, MB., M.Sc., Ph.D (Head of the Survey team)

The first three had worked in and knew the country well; to the others Africa was a new experience.

The original plan was for the team to spend the year surveying four villages, one urban, near Blantyre, one in the hills, (Jere's), one in the foothills, (Biwi's) and one on the Lakeshore (Kasamba), the last three being in the district of Kota Kota. In the event, though a start was made at the urban village of Ndirande, near Blantyre, in the Southern province, only the three villages of the Kota Kota district in the Northern province were surveyed in full, because of transport and communication difficulties. The Survey was also extended to eighteen months, from August 1938 to March 1940. A survey of the fish in Lake Nyasa, as suggested in the *'Nutritional Review of the Natives of Nyasaland'* was also carried out by two experts from

House lent to the Nyasaland Nutrition Survey (1938-40)
by the Dutch Reformed Church Mission at Chintembwe

England and an ADC, H. J. H. Borley, seconded from the Nyasaland administration.[5]

The co-operation of the villagers was obtained by remitting their hut tax for a year. Over the months there were changes of personnel; Dr. Read, early on, differed from Platt as to her role and thereafter conducted her investigations separately. Miss Owen found she could not combine her secretarial duties (for which she was not trained) with those of a botanist, her health broke down and she left after only a few months. She was replaced for eight months by Dr Geoffrey Herklots, Reader in Biology to the University of Hong Kong, who had a wide experience of tropical plants and had, like Platt, worked in China but not in Africa. The ever-mounting secretarial duties were taken over full-time by a married woman (Mrs Cran), recruited in Nyasaland, until the end of 1939, when the Survey was being wound up. When we arrived in January 1940 my wife helped on a part-time basis.

The headquarters of the Survey were at Chintembwe, near the hill village (Jere's) chosen for investigation. The large bungalow belonged to the Dutch Reformed Church Mission, whose married pastor lived close by. It was surrounded by a verandah which made the interior dark and cool and some of the rooms were interconnected. The tiny office at the end of the house also served as Mrs Cran's bedroom, access being either from the verandah or through the bedrooms, one of which was occupied by Jessie Barker (known as J. B. or Jabe). On one occasion Platt walked through to the office to fetch a paper, so deep in thought that he failed to notice that Jabe had returned early from her work and was taking a bath in the small round hip-bath with which we were all issued!

For relaxation there was a huge jig-saw puzzle laid out in the dining-room and padder, a modified form of tennis played with solid racquets, was played in the evening on a small court near the house. Presiding over the domestic arrangements was 'Momma' Platt, the slim, attractive wife of the Director, who ran 'The Plattery', as it was called, with great efficiency and tact; it was no mean task to cater for a fluctuating Survey staff and many, sometimes unexpected, visitors, in a place some 50 miles from the nearest store, and with a cook whose only words of English were 'Me know, me know', whether he did or not. The Platts had their third child with them, a toddler, having left the two elder children at home, My wife was then two months pregnant and I was glad to be able to leave her at The Plattery while I went down the escarpment to the Lakeshore to take over Kota Kota hospital and to get to know the district. It was the hot season, the rains had broken and the Lakeshore steamed unpleasantly.

By the time we arrived the members of the Survey team had dispersed, with the exception of Platt and Jabe, who as Nutritional Investigator, was helping to wind up the Survey. She was a small, slight, dark haired, very sunburnt woman in her early thirties, who had been educated at the North London Collegiate School, afterwards taking a 2nd Class Honours Natural Science Tripos, Pt. 1, at Newnham College, Cambridge. She taught botany for a year in a mining area in England during the depression and for another year (with maths) at a school in Hyderabad, India, an Indian Native State ruled by HEH the Nizam of Hyderabad. The school was for the daughters of wealthy high class Muslims. From there she moved on to a boarding school for the daughters of the wealthy in Mittagong, Australia, for two years, and returned home via New Zealand, Fiji, Hawaii, Vancouver and across N. America to New York. She sailed home across the Atlantic on one of the last trips made by the Cunard liner, Majestic, having been away for five years. Nowadays, such travels would excite no comment but in those days they showed considerable enterprise.[6]

Deciding to broaden her scope, Jabe spent two years studying for the Diploma in Dietetics. She then obtained a job as recorder on the Food Survey organised by Sir

The first dam built near Native Authority
Jere's village in Feb. 1939

Biwi's village in the foothills of the
Kota Kota district

Brewing beer at Biwi's village

Pot making

John (later Lord) Boyd Orr, working in London, Wisbech, Aberdeen, Dundee and West Wemys, and in 1938 was taken on as nutritional investigator of the Nyasaland Nutrition Survey.

Modest and unassuming, Jabe was an ideal person to be engaged as the member of any team living at close quarters in sub-optimal conditions where personalities sometimes clashed, and though of an easy-going temperament she always took the part of the under-dog. This, we considered, she sometimes carried to extremes. In a letter home, she wrote:

> 'I missed terrific excitement with a lion . . . much to my disappointment. We heard one day that a child in a village about 2 miles away had been taken and then after I left (Chintembwe), a message came at 6 o'c. at night that a woman in a village quite close had also been taken. It was too dark to do anything that night but next morning, Fitz (maurice), and Kettlewell and Parker (the DC at Kota) set forth and after a most exhausting time they arrived home triumphant with a poor skinny lioness about 10 o'c. The natives were very thrilled and did a dance and sang songs and there was great rejoicing. She apparently was half starved and scarcely bothered to try to get away . . .'

This *'poor skinny lioness'* had killed a woman and a child!

For over a year, while on the Survey, Jabe camped regularly in the three Survey villages, recording the heights and weights of the children and getting to know the families in each hut; what and when they ate and how they cooked the food; learning the native names of the various processes and the local names for all the plants identified by Dr. Herklots. The foods were then analysed and tables of food values prepared. She was popular in the villages and her sobriquet — for most Europeans were given one, some less flattering than others — was *'Mwadyachiani'* (what have you eaten?) for that was her first question on entering a village hut, after greetings were over. She had a great compassion for the women and their life of toil: the long hours spent pounding, sifting and cooking maize or cassava, carrying water, collecting fungi and leaves for cooking the 'relish' (*ndiwo* = lit. 'with it') which was served with the 'stiff porridge' *(nsima),* made of the pounded maize at the main meal, or drying the leaves *(mfutso)* for future use; spending many hours hoeing the gardens, planting maize and millet and waging war on the baboons, wild pig, francolin, guinea fowl, field mice and occasionally elephants, who threatened to destroy the crops. The women also brewed the beer provided as a reward for communal work (clearing of paths or bush, hoeing of gardens or for destruction of mischievous animals) in the villages. This nutritious beverage, made of maize and millet or cassava, gave a lift to village spirits with which she sympathised.

Her work complemented that of the Agricultural Officer, R. W. Kettlewell, who produced maps depicting the distribution of land in each village. These showed the huts, grainstores, graves, wells, paths, together with the crops grown in each district. He estimated, by sampling, the yield of crops grown, and made a study of the crop production methods employed, as well as the availability of *dimba* (moist valley) land and methods of using it. He also estimated the time spent on different crops during the year by each member of the family. He made a study of the social structure as affecting the allocation of land, the contribution made by domestic livestock to the rural economy and the customary practices governing the possession of cattle. He estimated the contribution to food made by tree crops (mango, *papaya,* bananas) and the customs governing 'ownership' of these and of 'bush' products such as honey. In addition to this he had the task of planning and opening up the trial plots at Mwera Hill, near Jere's village to test suitability for fruit and vegetable crops thought likely to improve the diet of the villagers.

1939 — Picking cassava leaves at Kasamba

Extra work had been put upon both these members of the Survey because it was at first thought that some of it was to be done by Dr. Read. Her terms of reference from the International Institute of African Languages and Culture, however, were much wider and did not include such detailed village studies and it was unfortunate that this question had not been settled in England before the Survey began its work. It would have saved unnecessary friction. William Rangeley, a young ADC, also contributed a very full account of native methods of traps and trapping of wild animals for he had extensive knowledge of African life in the bush.

The building of the first dam, which it was hoped would 'serve as a practical demonstration of the use of the Survey', was begun in February 1939 and Jabe wrote home:

> 'I think you would enjoy being here to help with the building of the first dam. It is very exciting, on Monday last (it is now Saturday), there was a peaceful valley with a maize garden covering most of it, by Tuesday after a day's work on the part of some 60 villagers, male and female, there was a wide road made through the bush to join the main road and a storm drain dug on either side of the valley to carry off water from the outskirts, a row of bamboos planted all round the prospective lake to hold up the banks, the position of the dam marked out and a vast amount of earth carted to start building the walls. Each day we have feared

Drying cassava roots

that the rain would come and wash everything away but by a miracle there has been none and now there is a mud wall faced with rock right across, about 4 ft. high, and a patch of water at least 2 feet deep and rising slowly but steadily, the dam when finished will be about 15 ft. high and the lake about 50 yards each way. There are to be two more quite close and the idea is that the land around will be properly irrigated and the lake full of fish for the villagers to eat. I am going down to Ķota tomorrow and on my return trip am to bring up various water plants and animals to get a food supply going for the fish. At present the whole countryside is being denuded of soil because the heavy rains wash it away as the trees have all been cut down with the result that soon there will be no decent land left unless something is done to stop the erosion. It is very important that the first dam should be a success just to show what can be done so both the chief engineers, Drs. P(latt) and H(erklots) have been having rather a wearing week especially when a storm starts blowing up.'

Platt had early on been an advocate of the idea that the Survey should be followed by a Nutrition development Unit, not just in one district but eventually all over the country, to carry out improvements and remedy the signs or suspected signs of malnutrition, which were being shown up by the Survey, and in a letter of the 29th March, 1939, Jabe reports:

'. . . One copy of the report (of the first six months work of the Survey) has actually gone, Mrs Cran was typing hard until the last moment and we hope that everything is in. It is a terrific thing, 9 sections and 22 appendices consisting of such things as copies of our various schedules, maps, notes on beer making, trees, etc. etc. . . . The last section deals with proposals for the future and if it goes through, as Dr. P. thinks it will, with the backing of Dr. O'Brien, the medical adviser to the C(olonial) O(ffice), it means a 3 year plan for Nyasaland

1939 Kasamba — pounding cassava roots

> or rather for this area and Dr. F(itzmaurice) and Kettlewell would carry on and I would stay out for I don't know how long teaching the women how to use the new foods that Kettlewell would show them how to grow. Already vegetables have been planted in the land below the dams which previously was a mass of reeds and now 4 dams are started . . .'

To Platt, in those days, nutrition was the panacea for everything. Familiar with the agriculture of China, where for forty centuries peasants had solved for themselves the problems of obtaining a living by increasingly ingenious methods of agriculture he held that those practices, so much more advanced than those of the Nyasaland Bantu, were the consequences of the better nutrition of the Chinese, and his fervour and his superior knowledge convinced many of us. But it was more likely that it was the result of forty centuries in which hunger was the penalty for failure to solve problems imposed by progressive increase in population density and in scarcity per head of land. Our Bantu had to date, lived a lean life, but nevertheless a life of sorts, by shifting cultivation; by cropping land continuously for years until its yield became insufficient, and then clearing and planting new land, enriched by the ash of burnt trees and other vegetation. They had yet to face situations where there was no new land, and Bantu wits and foresight had yet to be sharpened by necessity as had those of the Chinese. Platt ascribed their improvidence and inadequate, often wasteful, agriculture to malnutrition.

The Nutrition development Unit scheme soon ran into trouble with the Nyasaland Government. Platt's theory — that once shown the way, the Africans would grow more varieties of food, malnutrition would disappear and a new, healthier, more energetic population would succeed the present one — was the brain child of a young and eager man with no experience of Africa. The Nyasaland Government began to have cold feet, for he had failed to convince many of the senior officers of the soundness of his recommendations. Jabe wrote in July:

> 'They don't like anything new or having ideas that they should have had years ago, however, there will probably be such strong pressure brought to bear upon them that they will have to let the thing (the Unit) go on'. And she added: 'We are all a bit worried about what will happen if there is a war but from all accounts we are so well prepared now that Hitler will be a brave man if he risks it . . .'

I was as eager as Platt, and six years younger, and when I was appointed in January 1940 to the Nutrition Development Unit as its medical officer, I was excited, as I could see its tremendous potential. I had only been three years in the country in the Southern Province, but I was already dissatisfied with what I had observed and I knew that many of my fellow Furseians in the Administration felt the same. My wife had early on commented that the DCs and ADCs had only two subjects of conversation among themselves at 'sundowner' parties — the shortcomings of the Native Authorities with whom they had to deal and the lack of money to carry out any new schemes in their districts. We were now to be presented with a great opportunity and since the war seemed to be merely an affair of leaflet raids over Germany I was glad to be going to do what promised to be a worthwhile job.

I took my wife down to Kota Kota in March 1940 when the worst of the steamy heat was over and the Plattery was dispersing. Dr. Platt went off on a short visit to South Africa and 'Momma' with her daughter, and Jabe, with the copy of the final report (unfinished) to be delivered to the Colonial Office, travelled home by flying boat.

Medical Officer's house at Kota Kota

The Medical Officer's house was a double-storied building in Kota Kota, about half a mile from the Lake shore, mosquito proofed and uncompromisingly ugly, with the usual corrugated iron roof on which the rain drummed deafeningly in the rainy season. There was a Universities Mission to Central Africa station in the township, which consisted of about four thousand huts inhabited by the predominantly Muslim population, and a few Indian stores, scattered round about and along the old harbour.

The road leading to the Boma, and a belt of stunted *Brachystegia* trees, separated our house from the African Hospital and between the house and the road a coarse grass 'lawn' struggled to get its roots into a hard pan — part sand, part clay. At the back, some distance off and near the edge of the thin bush, were the boys' houses, nearer was a hen house which housed a few stringy native hens and two turkeys. All livestock lived a hazardous life. On one occasion a python entered our roost during the day, and, summoned by our boys, I found it in the act of squeezing a hen to death, too busy to notice me when I attacked and killed it with a hoe. On another, a leopard, breaking through the hen house thatch, made off one night with one of our fowls and then visited the DC, whose wife kept a superior breed of English hen. Warned by the commotion among the hens, the DC arrived with his rifle and, happening to look upwards, saw the head of the leopard on the roof of the hen house, outlined against the starry sky. At very close range he fired and killed it. This DC was a veteran of World War I, in which he had lost an arm, but he was a good shot nevertheless, and a very brave man. We also attempted to keep goats but they

Kota Kota — girl dressed for initiation ceremonies

became infected with the *Bacillus Abortus* of *Bang,* and had to be destroyed and eaten; meat was scarce so this was a windfall.

Rice, coconuts, cashew nuts, mangoes and other trees had been brought from Zanzibar by the Arab slave traders in the nineteenth century, but as vegetables were scarce, each of the four European households (the D.C., the A.D.C., the Clerk, Peter Hodgson and the M.O.) had a vegetable garden adjacent to a stream; ours was about a quarter of a mile away. Hot water for use in the house was carried from a hot spring nearby by the prisoners. Drinking water had to be boiled and filtered before drinking; this was a routine precaution all over the Protectorate and each household was provided with a filter. The 'candles' for the filter, and all provisions and household goods, were ordered by post from Blantyre and were sent up by the Lake steamer which called once a month at Kota Kota on its way up the Lake. Though Government provided basic furniture, married officers usually brought out extra pieces from England to add to the comfort of their homes. (My wife had been advised to bring out a bale of curtain material and a long mirror, which we did.) We had intended to buy a great many other comforts during our six months' leave, but as we left at less than a week's notice after only six weeks in England, we were unable to stock up and thereafter lived at a very basic level, especially since having been married abroad, we had not begun our wedded life with the usual mass of wedding presents. This was to prove an even greater handicap when we later set up house in an England of post-war shortages and rationing, not only of food.

I had been living a bachelor existence in Kota Kota since January, while my wife had been at Chintembwe and we expected a further separation in June. Our baby was due in July and had to be born in Zomba Hospital, 300 miles away. Regulations forbad European women to have their babies on an outstation. Not only was there no equipment to deal with obstetrical emergencies but the medical officers were employed primarily to serve the African population and could not be tied to their outstation headquarters. The procedure therefore was for the wife from up-country, (anything up to 600 miles away), to live with her husband's colleagues or other friends, in either Zomba or Blantyre for the four weeks preceding the expected date of birth and usually for a week or two after the 10-14 days spent in hospital.

After a few weeks together again in Kota Kota we obtained permission from the Director of Medical Services to attend the BMA annual dinner and dance in Zomba. It was an opportunity to meet friends and for my wife to shop for herself and the baby in Blantyre. We arrived late as the dirt roads were in their usual rough state after the rains and as we were dressing for dinner in a colleagues's house in Zomba, she began to have labour pains. I put her to bed immediately and they subsided but the next day she went into Zomba European Hospital for six weeks and then to another colleague's house returning to hospital on July 9th. Our son was born after a 'dry' labour, followed by a post partum haemorrhage, on the 10th, and I drove through the night from Kota Kota to find her exhausted, for there were no blood transfusions in those days. I returned to Kota Kota the next day and came down again to fetch her and the baby some three weeks later.

Though these events were personally traumatic they were nothing compared with what was happening during this period in the world outside, for shortly after the BMA dinner, Hitler stopped playing at war and began in earnest and disaster followed upon disaster for the British nation. France fell, the British Army was evacuated from Dunkirk and Britain seemed in imminent danger of being invaded and defeated. In Nyasaland each Government department pared its staff down to the bone and the young men were sent to join the King's African Rifles (KAR) in Kenya and thence to North Africa and the Middle East. From the Survey and Nutrition Unit went Bill Rangeley, Dick Kettlewell and John Dawkins (who had taken over from Dick Kettlewell) and, to our shame and disgust, John Borley the ADC at Kota Kota, and I were retained.

I wrote to Platt on the 6th July, 1940:

'Things are in the melting pot with a vengence now . . . Rangeley and Dawkins are now in Kenya and John Borley may or may not shortly be called. When the two former got their transfer I judged the Nutrition Unit was to die for the period of the war and applied for a transfer too, but was refused. One feels rather that one is fiddling while Rome burns, but the only thing to do is to determine to fiddle to some purpose . . .' and, having outlined my plans for the next year's work, I added:

'. . . you see the general plan. If I (and the Zomba MOs) could get a genuine line on tropical ulcer it would be some justification for playing such a pansy's part in this war . . .'

Notes and References

(1) The Assistant Director of Agriculture and Agricultural Chemist, A. J. S. Hornby, published 'An Agricultural Survey of Central Nyasaland' in 1935, and Dr H. G. Fitzmaurice wrote an article: 'Observations on the Native Foodstuffs, and Diet in the Kota Kota district' for the Annual Report of the Medical Dept. in 1936. In this he gave 'an account of the local foodstuffs, the method of preparing them, the weight of food eaten by a family of six persons over a period of 25 days, also some details of the weight of food eaten by 11 school girls during one week, with some observations on their development and nutrition.'

(2) The investigations and recommendations were:
(a) to determine the actual foodstuffs in use in native dietaries and their availability and values;
(b) to measure the supply of labour;
(c) to study the methods of production of native food crops and their relationship to the production of economic crops;
(d) to determine the effects of male adult emigration on village life'
and further that
'. . . To obtain a complete picture of present conditions, to have foodstuffs analysed and their nutritive values determined, to assess the amounts and availability of foodstuffs, their methods of cultivation, to determine how improvements may be effected, to bring home to the masses by education and propaganda the comparative values of staple foods and the advantage to be gained by an extension of the dietary in certain directions, will be the first steps in the general advance towards the improvement of general economic and health conditions.'
(Nutritional Review of the Natives of Nyasaland. 1938
Printed and published by the Government Printer, Zomba, Nyasaland.)

(3) International Institute of African Languages and Cultures. Founded in 1926, funded by the Rockfeller Foundation, to serve as a clearing-house for African information for the benefit of those engaged in official, missionary, or other work in Africa. In 1931 a five-year plan of research was launched to be directed to seeing the effect on African societies of their contact with European influences. Grants for study, while on leave, were made to officials or missionaries, as well as fellowships for full-time research to trained field workers.
(Hailey's African Survey, 1938. p.52)

(4) Beri-beri. The most common of all the nutritional diseases of the nervous system, is characterised by progressive weakness and muscle wasting.

(5) Report on the Fish and Fisheries of Lake Nyasa 1942. C.K. Ricardo Bertram, PhD., Ethelwyn Trewavas, D.Sc., H. J. H. Borley. Published on behalf of the Nyasaland Government

(6) Private papers.

Chapter 5

The definition of tropical ulcer is that it is a 'sloughing, pyogenic (pusforming) lesion, most common on the leg below the knee, usually associated with infection with *fusiform bacilli* and *spirochaetes.'* It was widely spread in tropical countries, and if not treated, scar contraction led to crippling deformities. By 1940 a certain amount of work had been done by nutritionists and other research workers, to try to identify its causes, with inconclusive results, and I decided to test Platt's theory that it might be due to a dietary deficiency. I began work on this in the Lake shore village of Kasamba and in a foothill village, Mbobo's. It was on the Kota Kota road and more accessible than Biwi's. A diagram was made of the legs of all the children in both villages and any abrasions on them were charted, week by week; if ulcers developed these were, of course, immediately treated. 1949 abrasions were followed through from start to finish for a year and if an abrasion yielded pus, the latter was examined, after Gram-staining, to determine the organism responsible.

Since no ulcers developed among the Lake shore children I then concentrated on Mbobo's, where I had found that more ulcers developed during the rainy season than in the dry. I decided to give one group of 40 children at Mbobo's a protein supplement in the form of meat, using another group at Mbobo's and one in a nearby village as controls. With a tracker, I shot an elephant, the meat was cut up and dried over large fires to preserve it, and about 4 oz. were later issued, boiled, to the Mbobo's children three times a week, giving an average 1.5 g. per kilo body weight daily of extra protein to each child. I also shot a hippo on the Lake shore and the meat, cut up and dried, was transported to Mbobo's to supplement the elephant meat. The tongue I reserved for ourselves, and I know of few more disconcerting experiences than to eat hippo meat under the disapproving eyes of our houseboys, to whom, as Moslems, hippo was forbidden. We also ate, or tried to eat, part of the elephant's trunk, but even minced, it defied our efforts to chew, such was its toughness! At Mbobo's there were one or two objections to eating hippo meat as it was alleged to cause leprosy.

At the end of the year there had been no improvement in the incidence of ulcer in the meat-fed children as compared with controls, but I had come to two conclusions as to why more ulcers developed in the rainy season. The first was that the abrasion scabs were more likely to be washed off when walking through the rain-sodden vegetation and so took longer to heal. The second was that a common muscid fly *(Musca sorbens)* was present in greater numbers during the rains. A test made with faeces, rotten fish, fresh blood and ulcer pus showed that the flies, though they might alight on the first three, quickly moved on to the ulcer pus. After half an hour there were 14 flies on the container of pus and none on the other containers. *Musca sorbens,* I therefore concluded, was a potential mechanical carrier of the organisms of tropical ulcer, infecting fresh abrasions from old infected ones. (Often one was first aware of fresh abrasions on one's hands or legs by the presence of a muscid fly feeding on the serous exudate.)[(1)]

In 1942 sinkings of ships by German submarines were frequent and our supplies of drugs etc. were depleted, but a small supply of yeast reached us. Jabe and I instituted a feeding experiment with it, to see if tropical ulcer would respond to massive doses of the B Vitamins contained in yeast. In order to find out the most palatable way of inducing the children to take it regularly, Jabe ate some herself and then unwisely swallowed some sugar to take away the taste. For the next half-hour she turned, in effect, into a highly productive factory of CO_2 gas, and it was therefore decided to boil the yeast before administering it to the children. The supply of yeast was only enough for the experiment to be carried on for five months (giving 1 oz. of yeast daily to each child). The results proved negative.[2]

The disease next to be studied as a possible effect of dietary deficiency was Vincent's angina, mainly affecting the gums from very early childhood. Known as *chiseye* (pronounced 'chi-sey-yeh'), it began, usually after weaning, as a condition of bleeding gums and persisted into adulthood, as pyorrhea and gingivitis, eventually giving a picture in old age 'of a few displaced teeth, almost hidden in chunks of tartar, joggling about in loose sockets from which pus wells'.[3] In childhood, after whooping cough or some other debilitating disease, *cancrum oris* (gangrene of the cheek) supervened, often as a terminal state.

It was thought, in view of the Nutrition Survey findings, that a shortage of Vitamin C in some months of the year might be the cause of this disease, but no cures were effected in spite of feeding patients for long periods with large quantities of boiled cassava leaf water, Cape Gooseberries or pawpaw juice (all rich in Vit. C).

These were the main areas of my medical research during the life of the Nutrition Unit, but there were various conditions reported by the Survey as probable or possible signs of malnutrition and minor vitamin deficiency states on which I also worked, until Dowa Hospital and district were added to my ordinary duties, when lack of time forced me to concentrate on Tropical Ulcer and *'Chiseye'* work. 'Visual purple' (dark adaptation) tests for Vitamin A deficiency, and skin conditions, especially *follicular keratosis,*[4] were two of them, but by 1941 I had begun to suspect that Platt's view of improvements in nutrition as a panacea for virtually all evils, was unfounded. We quite often had to follow a tracker over the twenty miles or so, which is about average distance even for experienced shots to cover for every wild beast killed in Kota Kota. I observed that men who might have skins with clear *follicular keratosis,* (which was also said to be indicative of Vitamin A deficiency), infected gums, and many other suspected manifestations of hypovitaminosis of one sort or another, were capable of remarkable endurance. The amount of caloric energy consumed seemed of considerable importance, and the amounts of vitamins of negligible importance, at least when considered in relation to the life and work of the Bantu and to their problems. In Nyasaland the importance of undernutrition was accentuated compared with malnutrition, because the farmer was inefficient, and mainly using an obsolete tool, the 'native' hoe.

(Post-war experience, from the researches of Ancel Keys and his co-workers, and from the sufferings of nations conquered and half-starved alike, have echoed this overwhelming importance of undernutrition compared with malnutrition in the Bantu world. The term *undernutrition* might with advantage be reserved for deficits in energy supply relative to energy output and *malnutrition* for qualitative (nutrient) deficit versus requirements. Henceforth I use these two terms in these special senses.)

Platt had been struck even more than we had by the differences in the pattern of disease and the novel and unusual diseases which the African showed compared with, for example, the Chinese who were also an agricultural nation. A further problem was that though these diseases might (or might not) be proved to be due to malnutrition, the causes of malnutrition extended into the very roots of the Bantu nation. To eliminate them involved a complete change of the nation itself. For example, it would be sensible to say that a hypothetical Vitamin C shortage could be much improved simply by planting the seeds or seedlings of various fruit trees which flourished in Nyasaland, but before they had reached more than a few feet high these fruit trees would be eaten by goats. The cure of Vitamin C deficiency therefore was to control the goats. But the control of goats involved either herding them or the construction of fences of stakes to protect fruit trees until they had grown out of reach, which involved continual watchfulness over a period of years. Thus the fundamental cause was a selfishness of the goat owners whose goats ate the trees. To combat this would involve either legal measures, through the Native Authorities, or a general public code of practice not to let goats stray through the village eating all the fruit tree seedlings.

One village headman, a forward-looking man, exasperated by the havoc wrought by these animals, forbade the entry of goats into the village. He built, instead, well protected accommodation for them at an adequate distance away. Within a few years, without the depredations of the goats, his village became a flourishing garden. Outside it, the stony seeds of guavas germinated in most favourable conditions, having passed undigested through the intestines of the villagers, much as the nuts of the borassus palms passed through the bowels of elephants to form the dense bush in which I had pursued them. Pawpaws flourished, mangoes grew and so did much besides. No other headman followed his lead, yet not a great deal of exercise of authority was required and the benefits were soon enough to be seen. The growing of fruit trees was merely a single example of one such chance neglected.

The medical research was, of course, only one facet of the Nutrition Unit's work and by no means the most important. The main object of the whole team was to work together to introduce new crops, to improve existing strains, and to introduce new agricultural methods and animal husbandry to the villagers. We were, however, hampered almost immediately by the curtailment of staff and restriction of funds which, because of the war, were cut down to a grant of £1,025 per annum for three years. This grant had to cover Jabe's salary, the erection of buildings on the site previously chosen (Mwera Hill) and the purchase of all necessary equipment.

Examining children — 1941
Jessie Barker and W. T. C. Berry in Jere's village

Bridge over the Kaombe River, Kota Kota district — 1941

Jabe arrived back in Nyasaland from England in September 1940. She lived in a tent in Jere's village until a house could be built for her at Mwera Hill, a couple of miles away, but we had no replacement for the agricultural officer, John Dawkins, for nearly a year, when Andrew Williamson was appointed as agricultural supervisor. The ADC for the hill area, Bill Rangeley, had gone to the war and was not replaced, and a house for me at Mwera was only built towards the end of the Unit's life, after Andrew Williamson had been housed there. There was no rest house in the area and I had either to camp, with all the extra car loads entailed, or stay with Jabe during the period.

A serious defect in the planning of the original scheme lay in siting the centre of the Unit's activities at Mwera, 65 miles away from the administrative centre and hospital at Kota Kota. Perforce, in doing official Government work, the DC and I had to spend much time at Kota Kota itself; there were, also, three European families stationed there with children, who might be at risk if I were not quickly available. The rough, earth road down the escarpment, through the tsetse belt, from Mwera to Kota Kota crossed the River Kaombe, and during the rainy season of

1940/41, the bridge over this river became unsafe for cars. Elaborate arrangements had to be made by wire (via Dowa and to and from Mwera by runner), for the DC or ADC, or both, to drive the 15 miles from Kota Kota to the bridge to pick up whoever was stranded on the other side. Nor was this the only potential delay, for between the Kaombe bridge and Kota Kota the road passed through the 'Onze', a small river running through a marshy plain, with reeds some eight feet high growing on either side of the road. To be 'stuck in the Onze' was a fate dreaded by all. There was a certain tree on the Kaombe side of the Onze — if the water had not reached the tree the road was passable, though the flood might be two hundred feet long or more in the rains. It was a question of merely driving on through the water; even on occasion blocking up all the orifices of the car with cotton soaked with grease, pushing the car through the water, and unplugging them the other side. A telegram once reached Platt saying 'Stuck in the Onze' which in transit became misprinted as 'Ooze', a very apt name!

In March 1941, Jabe and Andrew Williamson, in one car, and I in another, set off from Mwera for a Unit meeting at Kota Kota, (I had been working at Jere's). When we arrived at the Kaombe we found Bob Houston, then an officer in the Public Works Department (PWD), camped nearby, working on the bridge, but with his car on the Kota Kota side. Unable to cross we waited in the steamy heat while Houston drove in to Kota Kota to summon help, and Jabe wrote later: 'John Borley and Rob Allan came to the rescue, the former arrived, together with Houston, both mud from head to foot, having stuck in the Onze.' A fortnight later Jabe and I had agreed to meet at Mbobos to inspect the children there, but I had to wire her: 'Kaombe bad, Onze worse.' and she remained at Mwera. In other years even when the Kaombe bridge was repaired, the Onze remained a hazard during the rains.

At the Unit meeting in March our plans were thrown into disarray as a coded wire arrived instructing the DC, Rob Allan, to report to Khartoum without delay, to administer former (Italian) enemy territory. He left a week later and our new DC, Bob Keppel-Compton, was appointed early in April, a temporary 'drift' being made so that he could get his loads over the Kaombe River, the bridge being again unsafe!

The first year of the Unit's life had been a disappointing one. We had been able to do little but distribute seedlings of fruit and other trees among the villages, with attempts on Jabe's part at improvement in village dietary, and a very limited amount of soil erosion control and fishery work, and always with the thought that the Unit might be disbanded at any moment. Now that we seemed to be more secure, our plans became more ambitious.

An anti-erosion programme was organised and during Andrew Williamson's first year, 1500 gardens, supplying the food of some 5000 persons were protected from erosion. Since propaganda alone had proved useless in the past, the Native Authorities, (Chiefs Msakambewa, Jere and Kalumo), imposed legislation, sometimes somewhat ineffectively, each in his own area. The bunding was carried out by Africans trained by Andrew but every garden was inspected by him, since the nature of the terrain made it important that there should be no mistakes. The early clearing of the land, necessary for bunding, and thus the earlier planting of the maize on ridges, gave dramatic results. For the first time on record, Jere's people had a surplus of maize. The second year a smaller number of gardens were similarly treated because of the need to maintain supervision over the previous year's work. The need for continual supervision was high-lighted by the fact that of a fine piece of anti-erosion work carried out in the district by a previous Agricultural Officer, not a trace remained by the time Andrew began his work. However, to avoid the imposition of fines during this second year, legislation was replaced by propaganda to get land cleared in time for the first rains. A small number of people cleared their gardens early — the rest spent the crucial weeks drinking beer and dancing and had, the following year, the same miserable crops as usual.

While much time was spent on erosion control, work went on concurrently with the reclamation of swamp *('dimba')* lands. *Dimba* lands consist of colluvium deposited in the beds of vegetation-choked streams — reeds hold up silt and water washed down from the catchment area — and act as a sponge for the thirsty plains below in the dry season. In section, *dimbas* are triangular, the apex of the triangle extending down to the stream bed, the base, the reedy surface of the swamp, being more or less horizontal. When, as was happening everywhere in native agriculture, the vegetation was stripped off and gardens cultivated, the soil was washed away, deep gullies formed, eventually the stream dried up and an important source of water and a supply of food was lost. The Nutrition Survey had demonstrated that, by building dams along the length of a *dimba,* and irrigation, the amount and variety of crops, the fertility of the land, and the control of erosion, could all be increased. The Unit did not have the money to build dams on a big scale, but the reclamation work at Msakambewas, begun by the ADC, Dowa, (Colin Parker), before he was posted to military duties, was taken over and with constant supervision proved very successful, though there were difficulties initially. It was a large *dimba* and bamboo checks were put in to avoid scouring, functioning as small dams. These simple checks were resented by the cultivators because the water table was raised as a result and a close watch had to be kept to prevent their breaking them down or digging a channel round them. The crops grown, however, improved the diet, the surplus was sold, and the cultivators were later prepared to pay a small ground rent, sufficient to cover the cost of the supervision of the check dams by trained Africans, (about 1/- per year per garden was proposed). Eventually the *dimba* contained over 120 gardens, each of about 300 square yards, which produced excellent crops of peas, beans, pumpkins and other vegetables, as well as maize.

A second successful *dimba* reclamation was carried out in the foothills at Kasakula's. A *dimba* was drained outwards onto the hillsides. Erosion was controlled, and the sponge function of the *dimba* was preserved to such an extent that in one very dry year it was almost the only catchment stream of the Kasangadzi river still flowing. A whole village was settled onto the *dimba,* the produce from it added considerably to the variety in the diet and, incidentally, through the sale of surplus produce, the villagers acquired money for the first time, over and above their hut tax requirements.

Besides these two major *dimba* reclamation schemes there were many minor ones, each member of the Unit team preaching the gospel of soil conservation and distributing fruit and other tree seedlings (grown at Mwera and at the Survey dams) in the more remote villages when on *'ulendo'*. (This was the *Chinyanja* equivalent to on *'safari'* — each Administrative officer spent a week or ten days every month away from headquarters in camp, working in the remoter parts of his district.) Platt and Herklots had advocated during the Nutrition Survey, the introduction of exotic trees into the area, but the Forestry Department stressed the point to Williamson that these were impracticable as they were destroyed in the annual burning, so we then concentrated on fruit tree seedlings in the villages. This was not the only matter on which Departments differed from the Survey theories. It was pointed out that forest was the climax in the hills, therefore theoretically no cattle should be kept. Cattle keep down the grass so burning is unnecessary, but they are then crowded by the growth from old roots and hence erode the smaller area left to them, particularly the *dimba* lands. Part of the answer lay in planting permanent hedges to keep the cattle out of *dimba* land. Fifty per cent of the work done was spent on the annual repair of fences, but efforts to get the cultivators to plant hedges met with failure.

As we had been unable to include the original programme of cattle development in the Unit work, I only mention this as an example of the different interests which were involved and how they sometimes clashed. Some, though not all, of the 'obstructionists' of whom Platt complained were men who knew well the local conditions, the practical difficulties, and the results which might follow from pursuing another course.

Several thousand fruit tree seedlings were issued during the first year and six months later their fate was followed up. It was found they had suffered an 83% mortality, due to careless planting, lack of water and lack of protection from goats, so indiscriminate issue of seedlings was discontinued. We only gave them to villagers whose huts were well thatched and whose gardens were well cultivated — to give them to a slovenly household was a waste of time. The same thing applied when trying to improve the breed of native fowls, those scrawny African hens capable of supporting themselves without special feeding and wary enough to avoid the predators of the air and of the bush. If pure bred English birds were introduced into the villages, they required to be looked after and protected; a half-bred English cock running with native hens, we found, was the answer in trying to improve the strain.

On the Lake Shore, John Borley was concentrating on the construction of plank boats to replace dug-out canoes, a twine-making machine and a method for the better preservation of fish, besides the usual duties of an ADC. The plank boats were popular and were immediately bought at a price covering materials and wages of carpenters, (though copper nails and paint were unobtainable at that time) but no carpenter with a business sense could be found so that boat building had to be run as a European controlled affair.

Rope and twine making machines were constructed but they were not popular as they were regarded as involving work. Understandably the village method of rolling fibre on the thigh while sitting in the shade talking to friends was not considered work, but all too little twine was made by this method and nets were continually breaking. A better method of fish curing did not catch on becaused it involved mental effort and the curer could dispose of all his fish without it long before it went bad.

I noted in one of my reports: 'Nothing could possibly be done with Kota Kota fishermen save by compulsion', and by September 1941, John Borley decided that by the end of 1942 (when the Unit was due to close down unless given another span of three years), he would have shown the natives as much as he could and if they hadn't started to show interest by then they never would.

On the other hand Jabe had successfully interested several men and boys in the art of spinning the local cotton.[(5)] An ex-prisoner, alleged to have been a murderer, ('he doesn't *look* like a murderer' she remarked typically to us on his arrival!) was sent from the Southern Province to teach others to spin, and with much difficulty a loom also was constructed at Mwera with heddles made from John Borley's fine string. By next May there were two spinners and she had taught several women to knit, using sharpened bamboo sticks as knitting needles. Propaganda at Visanza tobacco market with a boy spinning and women knitting, aroused interest. Eventually several men and boys were spinning in a hut at Mwera; it was popular work because it produced cash and could be done in company. The first dye she used was made of dried tea dust, giving a dirty khaki colour, but later she was able to experiment with dyes obtained from Johannesburg in South Africa.

One other innovation which was popular was the introduction of wheat as a cash crop. Fifteen men were persuaded reluctantly to try it the first year, for Nyasaland was aiming to become self-sufficient in wheat in wartime, and though it did very badly, they were able to sell the small amount harvested. The next year we were interested to hear that one hundred men had *asked* for seed. Rye, which was also tried, did very well but as it was not a cash crop and the *'nsima'* it made when pounded and cooked was reckoned to be too sweet and not stiff enough, the villagers were not interested in growing it.

By the end of 1941 the members of the Unit were agreed that we were proceeding on the wrong lines. Compulsion, propaganda or education were none of them the way to get our ideas over, but we had discovered men in the bush, who without any of these forces were forging ahead on their own. These were the progressive men, the individuals with foresight and initiative, like the village Headman mentioned earlier. These men did not have to be compelled to clear their land early; they looked after seedlings; they grew and protected fruit trees. One such was Kosam, whose flourishing garden, hidden away in the bush, Andrew Williamson discovered by accident when on *'ulendo'*. His *dimba* was a garden of Eden and had been begun as far back as 1927. It was in a lovely valley, opened up with main and side drains with hundreds of fruit trees, bearing well — oranges, peaches, apples, guavas, together with maize, beans, tomatoes and many other sorts of vegetables. 'Much better than anything we can do', wrote Jabe candidly. None of his neighbours had profited by his example and in fact he was the object of so much jealousy and envy that he had had to move out of his village and live elsewhere. (Possibly because he had broken with the tribal tradition and refused to feed his more improvident relations during the seasonal shortages.) Kosam and the very few like him — I referred to them in a report as *'good deeds in a naughty world'* — amounting to perhaps one in ten thousand of the population, were eager to try new ideas and new varieties of crops. One man said to me: 'Come round my garden and if there is anything I need to do, I will do it.' There was nothing.

We had found in the district that if *we* supplied the necessary initiative to set up a project which needed either some measure of preparation in advance or some initial spark of drive or of organisation, most of the Bantu would follow us, but they all too often seemed to lack the capacity to maintain the project against the wear and tear of time and use. They saw the point of erosion control and its results, but good work done by our predecessors had not been sustained and all trace of their work had disappeared. Good harvests attended our drive for contour ridging and early planting but the impetus was not sustained against the appeal of jollifications during the crucial period. The local strain of fowl was a poor layer but it had developed the capacity to *survive neglect* and no specific feeding during the periods of food shortage. In fact the African had much in common with his domestic animals when it came to surviving the recurrent food shortages which were a common feature of increasing pressure on the land. (From children at the height of the 'hungry season', *'Mwadyachiani'* would often receive a brief reply: 'Today is not my day for eating.') One of John Borley's pupils neatly hit the nail on the head when he said: 'Your plank boat is much better than my dug-out canoe, but it requires repeated looking after in a number of small ways, whereas my old canoe does not. And if I neglect it, it still is usable for my fishing, where your plank boat would not be.'

The African recognised his own faults and weaknesses and when they rebounded upon him, to his credit he did not whine about them but admitted them with a sort of mock humour. Near a Dutch medical missionary, a friend of mine and a very good doctor, lived a man whose habits were so lazy that 'even among his fellows', said my friend, with a mixture of affection and exasperation, he was nicknamed *"Ulesi"* (pronounced as you might expect). During one exceptionally lean season my friend explained to him that he was now experiencing the fruits of his idleness. 'Yes,' said the man, 'those who didn't work are hungry . . . but the ones who have worked, they are hungry too . . . so why work?' My friend had a sense of humour and *Ulesi's* reaction was so typically African that it was difficult to sustain the attitude of the 'unco guid'!

Though the bulk of the population were held back, not by ignorance, but by lack of foresight and ambition, it had to be remembered that we were dealing with a residual population. The cream of the people had emigrated, some to the mines in South Africa or Northern Rhodesia and some to work in other territories. The sprinkling of ambitious men discovered by one or other of us while on *'ulendo'* in the district, had found it was more profitable to stay at home and sell food to the dependents of emigrants. We thought that a register of such men should be compiled, eventually in every district, so that a district officer taking over a new station would know who were the intelligent individuals to contact. These men were the channel by which we could best hope to touch the mass of the people but it would take a long time and in the meantime the population was increasing. Though agricultural erosion in the area had been reduced, erosion due to stock, and loss of water storage due to deforestation, continued. We felt the efforts of the Unit would be rendered futile unless long-term legislation covering land planning and pasture management were introduced and sufficient staff provided to enforce it. This would, under the existing system, have to be done through the Chiefs, acting as Native Authorities, as I have set out in the previous chapter.

After much thought, Bob Keppel-Compton and I wrote a report in 1942 on our failure to make a success of Platt's recommendations and advised that there were certain necessary measures which were unsuitable to be enforced via Indirect Rule. This report we sent to the authorities in Zomba, I, at least, naively thinking that we were drawing something to their attention of which they were not aware. In fact, however, the authorities were all too well aware of the difficulties and were trying to combat them, using the mask of Indirect Rule. This was partly done, I felt, that they might claim kudos for yet another extension of the system and partly, in complete good faith, because Indirect Rule had indeed *'become sanctified by its own success'* and was *'being reverently . . . prolonged . . .'* To our lords and masters it must have been as gall and wormwood to have to read our pedantic expositions on the subject! 'K-C' was a man of great moral courage. He could see that our report spelt trouble both for himself and others but held that things were said in it that ought to be said, and fearlessly sent it in.

The explosion was not long in coming. He was sent for to Zomba and reprimanded by the Governor, who accused him of disloyalty; to which K-C replied that his loyalty was to the Protectorate and that he stood by all that was written in the Report. I was visited by my Director of Medical Services (a successor to Dr. de Boer, who had been posted to Uganda) and firmly though tactfully 'ticked off'. A few months later the Nutrition development Unit came to the end of its three year term and the grant was not renewed.

Notes and References

(1) Tropical Ulcer: Studies in its Causation, by W. T. C. Berry, M.A., M.B., D.T.M. & H. (Excerpt from the Journal of The Royal Sanitary Institute, Vol. LXIX, No. 5, September, 1949)

(2) The effect of a yeast supplement to the diet. From the Final Report on causes of Tropical Ulcer arising from work done with the Nutrition Unit, Nyasaland. (Enc. No 1 in Nyasaland No 62 Saving of 28/7/44. Dr. W. T. C. Berry. In the London School of Tropical Medicine & Hygiene, among the Nyasaland Survey papers)

(3) Nutrition Unit Medical Section: Interim Report 1941. (In the London School of Tropical Medicine & Hygiene, among the Nyasaland Survey papers)

(4) Follicular keratosis: Enclosure in a letter to Dr Platt dated 30/1/43 (In the London School of Tropical Medicine & Hygiene among the Nyasaland Survey papers) Follicular keratosis gives the skin a feeling of roughness like a nutmeg grater.

(5) Cotton spinning. 'In 1876 it was quite common to see in villages on the Shiré young men and old men busy spinning cotton into thread; and below a shady tree . . . would be an old man weaving a piece of cloth on a loom which he had made himself.' (Sir) Harry Johnston observed that the importation of European cloth almost destroyed the African weaving industry.' Quoted by Bridglal Pachai in 'Malawi: The History of the Nation', Longman Group Ltd., London, 1973. p. 163.

Chapter 6

Between 1940 and 1943, besides the activities of the Nutrition Unit described in the previous chapter, I was also Medical Officer in charge of both Kota Kota and Dowa districts, an area about the size of Kent and Sussex, whose hospitals were nearly ninety miles apart. The Witwatersrand Native Labour Association (WeNeLa) stationed a number of their officers at Dowa to recruit labour for the South African mines and I was helped by the doctor on their staff who spared what time he could from his own work to deal with emergencies when I was elsewhere. He was a good chap, a South African, but a stranger to the ways of life by which we were carrying on through the war years in Nyasaland.

One day in Kota Kota I had an emergency call from him at Dowa. A woman had been admitted about a fortnight before with an apparently superficial head wound from an axe, (administered, I believe, by her husband), and had done well on conservative treatment until that morning, when she had abruptly lost consciousness and had not regained it. From his description on the 'phone there seemed to be some intracranial complication, conceivably a haemorrhage, though in view of the fourteen days' interval an intracranial abcess seemed more probable. I said I would come up. Arrived there (over some 87 miles of rough road), he admitted that he had no instruments for skull surgery at Dowa, and had assumed that I usually travelled from hospital to hospital with these — a reasonable assumption, I blame myself for not thinking of it. The woman was indeed deeply unconscious and on probing in the depths of the wound there was an underlying fracture of its vault. Instruments or no instruments I could not drive a further 174 miles of Rift Valley road before dawn next day by which time she might well be dead. Therefore we visited the African station carpenter and selected from his tools a large, widely curved chisel (or should it be called a gouge?). Also a mallet. These we autoclaved.

Having placed the patient on the operating table, still unconscious, I fell to. Being unconscious, she needed no anaesthetic and having exposed the fracture in the vault of her skull I chiselled at it with the zeal of a South Sea Island medicine man trepanning his subject. The wider the area over which I removed bone away from the axe wound, the more she began to show signs of recovering consciousness until, after maybe half an hour, I had fully exposed the underlying covering of the skull and she had to be lightly damped down with anaesthetic.

Months later as I was sitting by a roadside in the heat of the day, a woman approached me. 'Do you know me?' she said. 'I remember you'. 'Who am I?' (This with a sceptical grin). 'I remember your face, not your name.' 'What do you remember?' 'I remember the work I did on your head. Come nearer.' So saying I turned her round and parted her hair. There, sure enough, was the healed scar of the long cut I had made in order to approach the site of the axe wound in her scalp to chisel it open with the station carpenter's tools. 'It's *very* painful', she said with a look that belied her words. 'That' I said firmly, 'is a *very* great lie.' The roar of laughter that came from the bystanders and from the woman herself, told me a good deal. She was obviously a great tease and known as such. I thought she might well have gone a little too far in teasing her husband and he had in exasperation clouted her with his axe. Whether he would have been successful in pleading justifiable homicide, had it not been for my exploits with carpenter's tools I do not know. I confess I was surprised at finding nothing of import at operation, but I expect that there had been an underlying oedema of the brain which was relieved as soon as I had opened it up.

One day a fisherman was brought to my hospital at Kota Kota with a mangled arm after an encounter with what, in the Book of Job, is called 'the king of beasts'. 'The crocodile is the king of beasts' and in the Bible the afflicted Job is exhorted to consider the crocodile as having royal power because he siezes his prey and none can oppose him. So also it is with the all-powerful Lord whose impositions must be borne without complaint; not, perhaps, an attitude wholly in line with modern thought and not, perhaps, shared by the victim.

It had occurred in one of the many streams which, rising in the foothills of the escarpment forming the left wall of the Rift Valley, meander through the green fringe of reed and weed that flanks the shore of Lake Nyasa, forming channels in which fish abound. So too, do the crocodiles that feed upon the fish. If a fisherman should set a line of fish traps across the channels, and should a crocodile encounter it in his leisurely search for fish in the stream, it often makes no attempt to break through but just waits, almost imperceptible below the surface, perhaps for days, eating any fish that happens to come his way, and waiting upon the turn of events. One day he is rewarded by the spectacle of the fisherman, his arms almost shoulder deep in water, feeling for any fish that may have been caught within his traps. The tempo then abruptly changes, as with a single furious rush, often smashing the bones of the arm into several fragments, the 'king of beasts' upsets the fisherman out of his canoe and bears him, mangled and half-drowned to be stored underwater and eaten at leisure. In this case the other men in the canoe, quick of wit and stout of heart, hammered with their paddles at the beast's head and hauled their companion into safety; and then began painful days of porterage north along the Lake shore to my hospital, so painful that when I said: 'the arm must come off', the patient at once agreed.

The arm revealed itself at operation as little more than a bag of pus, with fragments of broken bone lying in it. The main artery of the arm had clotted, but to remove the arm the artery had to be tied and cut, which was done by means of a separate incision as far away as possible from the infection around the crocodile bite; as it was done I said that if it were to become the site of secondary haemorrhage 'there would be hell to pay', as it would become necessary to explore the upper reaches of the arm in order to re-tie the main brachial artery (or even the sub-clavian artery).

All went well for a fortnight or so. Then one morning the dresser in charge of the ward reported that the wound was bleeding and, as I watched, large drops of blood issued, about one per half second. There was, now, an indication of 'hell to pay.' The clot in the main artery, (which runs down the length of the arm) was beginning to shift.

I gave the man a dose of morphia and bound his wound. Morphia would relieve the pain and calm the patient and so there would be less tendency to bleed. But if it were insufficient to reduce the haemorrhage, then a crucial moment came, the point of no return; for the patient would have lost so much blood that he could not stand anything in the way of prolonged surgical interference. Even then the case was not hopeless if the surgeon were quick and experienced and the artery easily approached. So there was a moment for decision: *when* to go in. I left orders for the operating theatre to be prepared for an emergency in one half hour and in the meantime I returned to the house to consult my surgery books. This is a measure which the bush surgeon — and God knows I can only style myself a surgeon by necessity — must never neglect. Even in operations with which he is familiar he is liable to find some special point in relation to the case in hand which he might not have borne in mind. It was around eleven o'clock and my wife was holding a morning tea party for the three other European wives of Kota Kota. The layout of the room was such that I could approach the book that I wanted by crossing it, stepping over the legs of all three, too deeply immersed in thought about the impending operation to pay heed to — even to be conscious of — any of them or their greetings. I have a dim recollection of bare legs, of which my only impression is that there were too many of them, as I groped in the wooden petrol box that did duty as a bookcase at the end of their array and returned, book in hand, leaving my wife to repair as best she could the ruins of her party.

The book held little comfort for me. There were two possible approaches to the subclavian artery which is what I must tie off: (i) above the clavicle and (ii) below. About (i) it said: 'This is an approach normally only taken by the experienced competent surgeon.' 'Not me', I said, and at once went to (ii), described as 'a surgical exercise normally only carried out on the corpse.' And, by God, before I was through I began to realise what they meant! But I was saved by a brilliant anaesthetic given by my hospital assistant, Dan Ngurube, who kept the patient 'alive but not kicking', what time I groped desperately in the depths of the wound and tied the artery off.

About three to four months later I was crossing a maize garden on the shore of Lake Nyasa, well south of Kota Kota, when the patient came running across to me. I knew him by his missing arm and by the remnant of it that projected from his shoulder. He was in fine trim, probably cared for by his family or relations. He said that what was left to him of his arm, when I had finished with it, was quite useful, for with it he could manage in some sort the long handle of a tool gripped in his other hand. He made no mention of manipulating fish traps again below the surface of the water and I was in no way eager to repeat my incursion into the field of expert surgery.

You will notice that I only describe cases with a happy outcome. I would not have you imagine me a better surgeon than I am — there have been other, less happy, outcomes, but I find it more consoling not to dwell on these. The fact is, if a doctor penetrated deep among the shy and suspicious peasants of his 'bailiwick' and won their uncritical trust he was liable to be confronted with many situations like these. A budding surgeon becomes expert only by the practice of his craft and is a specialist; but in England he usually has with him an experienced colleague to 'hold his hand' should he falter in unfamiliar ground, and who helps him through. In 'Darkest Africa' it was not so. The decision, to go in or not to go in was made, not by a specialist surgeon, but by an ordinary medical officer and was made alone and was irrevocable. Usually the doctor knew the task to be within his powers and the question did not arise; or it may have been possible to convey the patient to the care of some more skilful surgeon. If the doctor were approachable by nature his Hospital Assistant might help him. I recall on one occasion I was studying a patient with a tumour of uncertain origin in her neck. My Hospital Assistant, the wise and courteous Marko Mpelele, with experience both of my limitations as well as my skills, read the question in my mind and remarked quite casually: 'I shall be pleased if we do not do this one.' So we didn't do that one.

Working at Jere's and staying at Mwera Hill with Jabe, I received a message one day asking me to call on a sick 'bambo' who thought he had *'nkufi'*. *'Nkufi',* a tick, is relapsing fever which affects men who travel much by road and sleep in infected rest houses. 'Ticks do not bite those with bad blood' remarks, or in my day did, the admirable *Chinyanja*-English dictionary of the Reverend Alexander Hetherwick. With dry Scottish humour the Reverend Alexander adds: 'A great consolation to those who are bitten.' A 'bambo' is a Marist (RC) priest and this one admitted that he had been bitten, seeming to find only limited consolation from the Reverend's observation. He had a temperature of 103° and I took him in my car to the small European hospital at Lilongwe, some 50 miles away. It was the rainy season and on the way we passed a long sheet of shallow water with some men working beside it; not much different from what one meets in England at times when the rainfall temporarily exceeds the capacity of the outlet to drain it. So long as the driver proceeds slowly and the water is not so deep that it obstructs the outlet of the exhaust there is no problem. About half-way over, my front wheels unexpectedly lost contact with the road and the car subsided gently into a ditch which the gang had dug across the road to drain away the flood water and which could not be seen from the surface.

The gang apologetically lifted my front wheels out of the ditch and all would have been well but for a peculiarity of the Chevrolets of that time to have the battery positioned under the floor boards, so that the base of the battery was the nearest thing to the ground. Then, as in this instance, the first warning that all was not well was that the battery was forced up through the floor boards, wrenching at its connections in its ascent. I do not know exactly what went wrong with the battery, but it then lacked the power to turn the self-starter but could maintain the engine ticking over provided the car was pushed sufficiently fast to start it when pushed in gear. This the labour gang was well able to do and the Bambo and I parted with them, the Bambo along with his *nkufi* and I with thanks, and messages for God Speed (or its *Chinyanja* equivalent). All went well for twenty miles until we approached the summit of the pass which led downhill to hospital and to rest for the Bambo. But at that point the road proved unnegotiable and the engine died. 'If you will sit in the driver's seat, Father,' I said, 'I will push until we are over this little rise and all will be well.' 'Alas!' he said, 'I cannot drive.' 'I fear then, that you will have to push, for I forsee no car on this road before night falls.' So the unfortunate Bambo, relapsing fever and all, had to push and I must say he did it manfully. We arrived in due course at Lilongwe Hospital, the Bambo's sole concern being that by staying at the hospital until he was well, as I insisted he must, he would be running up a terrible bill for his Mission to pay.

A week or two later I received a letter from him saying he was getting better and his superiors had not taken him to task for his enforced extravagance, as I knew full well they would not. I merely mention this instance to illustrate the stern discipline that they observed — or at least which the Bambos thought they observed, which is not the same thing at all! These Bambos were Roman Catholic priests, mostly from French Canada, humble, devout peasants, robust and confident in their faith which, in its simplicity and clarity, is akin to the Muslim faith, as also is the strictness with which it is observed by believers. I understand that when posted to Africa they bade their friends and relations farewell, for it was unlikely that they would return except for quite exceptional reasons and only after many years of service.

For Government Servants the usual six months' leave in the United Kingdom after a two and a half year tour, had been suspended for the duration of the war and we were sent to South Africa for three months instead. Between leaves, during each hot season, the European wives on the Lakeshore moved up to the hills. One year my wife lived in the vacant ADC's house at Dowa, while the other Unit wives went to Nchisi, about five miles from Chintembwe. In 1941, while the others went to the hotel at Dedza, my wife and baby son, then aged 15 months, spent some weeks on their own in Chief Mbobo's two-roomed resthouse.

Early in December a messenger reached me in Kota Kota with a note to say that the baby was ill. I drove up and fetched them both down to Kota Kota — the baby had a high temperature and that night had a convulsion and nearly died. He was suffering from cerebral malaria but the injection of quinine I had given him earlier saved his life. Babies were given liquid quinine daily in malarial districts but cases of malaria were all too frequent, and were not confined to the children. Europeans at

Kota Kota (and in other low-lying malarial districts) got it. We all took quinine tablets daily, they were regularly placed on the dinner table, passed round before the soup and offered to any guest who happened to be there. We wore mosquito boots in the evening and we slept under mosquito nets, though the houses were mosquito proofed, but we were bitten, either in the house or on *ulendo* in spite of these precautions and most of us suffered recurring bouts of malaria, though for various reasons blackwater fever was almost a thing of the past.

Our baby son was very ill for the next few days and was made worse by prickly heat and by the fact that I had to remove thirty *'putsis'* from his napkin area. The *putsi* fly lays its eggs on laundry hung up to dry, but the eggs are killed if the garment is well ironed. If this is inadequately done the eggs hatch out into maggots on contact with the body. These burrow under the skin and have to be squeezed out, a very painful process.

These days of anxiety and stress coincided with the attack on the American fleet at Pearl Harbour by the Japanese, but we scarcely took in the event when John Borley came round to tell us of it. Either he or K-C had a battery-operated 'wireless' set on which we depended for our news of the war. Otherwise we read it in the Central African Times (the 'CAT'), which was brought once a week by runner from Dowa, together with our mail and a pound of butter, runny and sometimes rancid in the hot weather.

Our second son was born in Zomba Hospital in June 1942 and six weeks later we were sent on our three months leave, travelling down to South Africa in a train packed with troops. I had been suffering for some months from a recurrence of the dysentery I had contracted in 1939 and this persisted after my return. It was owing to this that when the Unit closed down I was posted full-time to Dowa hospital and a refugee Jewish doctor took over at Kota Kota.

For a few months my belly became so tender that I had myself carried around Dowa hospital, sitting in a modernised version of a sedan chair. While on one such round I met an African bearing a badly mauled puppy. 'It has been bitten by a mad dog. What shall I do?'' 'Kill it,' I said and organised a gang with implements to kill the mad dog if it could be found in the township. I sent word to the house to warn my wife, who was entertaining Jabe, in Dowa to see the D.C. on business, to shut both pets and children up, safe in the house, from the mad dog. After an hour or so the gang returned having failed to find it. 'I think the dog belongs to the European who is visiting your house,' ventured the owner of the bitten puppy. I joined my wife and Jabe, laughing. 'They say *your* dog is mad!' I told her. 'Well', she replied rather guiltily, 'she has been behaving oddly.' Our son of two had had a superficial bite on the nose when the dog had arrived and jumped up at him. A quick round-up of pets revealed the kitten with a bad bite, fortunately our dog had been with me. Jabe's dog was skulking under a bed and we put it in the back of the car and drove it to the vet's office in Lilongwe, about thirty miles away. The vet advised that the dog should be kept in the pound and in transferring it Jabe was bitten and my hands wetted with saliva.

The problem of rabies had been vastly reduced by the introduction of the Pasteur vaccine, indeed I had only heard of one case since in Nyasaland. The vaccine, however, was unpleasant, consisting of a dozen or so large injections, ideally into the skin of the belly, and I left the treatment of our son to a colleague in Lilongwe, my own course was administered by my wife (not a nurse), and Jabe, I delivered to the care of Andrew Williamson at Mwera. The dog died the following day in the pound and the brain was reported as positive for rabies. Some time later we had a letter from Jabe to say that she was well: 'And guess what — I'm going to marry Andrew!' Love burgeons in the strangest circumstances!

Owing to the critical report that K-C and I had written we were neither of us regarded with favour by our superiors at this time. I had been very sorry to lose Dr de Boer, who left for Uganda before we sent in our report and who, as Chairman of the Native Welfare Committee was interested in, and backed us in the Nutrition Unit. He had drive and was a very efficient Director of Medical Services. He had made a tour of the outstations soon after his arrival in 1938. He then wrote a Memo to the effect that such was the poverty of Nyasaland as a Protectorate that the medical services, however willing, could not function efficiently — a tree with sparse roots and starved leaves was his analogy — and that his staff, of all ranks, were housed in many cases, and especially in the outstations, in accommodation unsuited to the climate or conditions.

At that time it was the practice for District Commissioners to submit, (presumably to the Secretariat?) Annual Confidential reports on district Medical Officers. Replying, with cordial thanks, to a routine Memo from the Chief Secretary asking if he wished the practice to continue, he is said to have gone on to suggest that Annual Confidential reports on District Commissioners should also be submitted from Medical Officers. I understand that the practice was then dropped!

During their time in Nyasaland, he and his wife, Essie, kept open house for all their medical officers coming through Zomba from up-country. They housed for long periods the wives of the MOs who were with the Army in North Africa; they also offered hospitality to the wife of any medical officer waiting to have a baby in Zomba European Hospital.

Dr de Boer's successor was a serious, very efficient man, determined to render the service more effective: humourless, and, by me, much disliked. Nevertheless he got into my consciousness the concept that one could, by not being too blunt in one's condemnation of the system, achieve one's ends without in turn exciting reprisals. A very experienced planter once told me: 'When I see a bright lad with original ideas, I give him five years. By that time he is either *in,* by which I mean *broken in,* or he's *out,* by which I mean . . .' I assured him I knew what he meant and remembered this conversation when the Unit closed down. I began to make enquiries where else I could go. I recall — and for the first time — a smile on my new Director's face when I later told him of my decision to seek some other colony: 'Of course, you ambitious young men . . . etc. etc.' and he heartily wished me well.

After five months at Dowa I was posted to Zomba to take the place of the Government Pathologist while he went on leave to South Africa. We found conditions there very different from Kota Kota. We lived in the Pathologist's house and his beautiful garden on the slope of Zomba mountain was irrigated from a mountain stream — it was the sort of house that a junior Medical Officer could not aspire to for many years. There were stores too, in Zomba, though the goods on the shelves were scanty as many shipments from the United Kingdom had been sunk by German submarines, and the substitutes from South Africa and Southern Rhodesia were not of the same quality as the English goods. Butter, milk and meat, however, were readily obtainable. The Club was large and there were dinner parties for which people wore evening dress and the King's African Rifles' officers and serjeants provided a certain amount of gaiety and new faces. We noticed that car tyres were less worn than those in use up-country, though we, ourselves, sported nearly new tyres on our old Chevrolet Coupe Imp. This was because, when Dr de Boer had visited me in Dowa, he had suffered with me nine punctures on the 110 miles of road to Salima and back. A whole shipload of tyres had recently been sent to the bottom by a German submarine, but as he left he said to me: 'There are a few tyres kept in Zomba for Very Important People — like me! I will see what I can do.' He was as good as his word, five new tyres arrived shortly afterwards which lasted me till the end of the war, and reduced the problems of travel on both myself — and my houseboys.

In spite of the fleshpots of Zomba, however, my wife and I both preferred the three months we spent at the Scotch Mission Hospital outside Blantyre, to which we were posted after Zomba. The staff consisted of two European doctors, a European sister and numerous dressers being trained up to Hospital Assistant standard. The hospital had a deservedly very high reputation with a very skilful surgeon at its head.

Accompanied by the Sister, I left a ward gloomily one day. A patient wasn't doing as well as I had hoped or expected and this depressed me. 'You're thinking about that man,' said Sister S. accusingly, 'but you've worked here for two and a half months and this is the first of your patients that hasn't done well. Think about the others for a change and you'll feel better.' I did so, and I did feel better. Sister S. was a darling. Brunette, petite, devout, always working, always cheerful, only one thing put her out: to see her medical staff treating their patients without the kindness and care which is the essence of Man's humanity to Man, and which also constitutes good nursing. When that happened her eyes would flash with indignation, and her cheeks flush with wrath (which made her look very pretty, incidentally). 'Oh, I could have clocked him one' she would burst out, and one listened sympathetically, knowing well that nothing, nothing, could really have made her 'clock' him one — or if the inconceivable happened and she did so do, she would be buried in self-reproach for a fortnight. Dear Sister S!

One day she told me of a conversation she overheard, behind 'the screens'. In response to something derogatory from a medical dresser, the patient, an elderly man (and as such entitled to expect respect from other Bantu) burst out with: 'Why can't you learn to do as your doctor does? He has far more healing knowledge than you, and yet he would never have spoken to me as you have done.' This patient might either have been speaking of me, or of the Mission doctor, who was always courteous and kind; to this day I don't know which, though I took myself sufficiently seriously to watch myself in the following weeks, during which I was neither guilty of discourtesy nor had consciously to refrain from such (and anyway if I had been, Sister S. would clocked me one!) I think one of the dressers, who, puffed up with the conceit of a little learning, had forgotten Christ's 'Love thy neighbour as thyself.'

Our future after Blantyre was uncertain. On the children's account my wife was fearful that we should be posted to an unhealthy outstation, and it was a great relief to her when we were then sent to Cholo, another area of tea plantations, south of Blantyre. Here we were happy to welcome Jabe, who in 1943 had married Andrew Williamson. He had obtained a transfer to the Leeward Islands on the closure of the Unit, but the ship on which they were to travel to the UK refused Jabe a passage as she was pregnant. She came to stay with us at Cholo until the baby was born (my wife was also pregnant with our third child) but passages were so difficult to obtain that it was very many months before she obtained one. We referred to her after that as the guest who came for a week and stayed a year!

In Cholo hospital I met again the Hospital Assistant whom I disliked. His surname was the same as that of a formidable Boer general, and his manner was in keeping. Whether some of the antagonism between Boer and Briton had rubbed off during his period of education and training as a Hospital Assistant, I do not know, the Mission where he received it was a Dutch one. On my first arrival in Nyasaland, he rarely made any positive move to acquaint me, as a newcomer, with the ropes, whereas in subsequent years I learnt a lot from the excellent Hospital Assistants of other hospitals. When therefore, he and I confronted each other again at Cholo hospital, I made sure that we established a proper relationship from the start. I told him that, having had a year or two's experience with other Hospital Assistants, I had come to realise how negative and unhelpful his attitude had been when he and I had first worked together, and that it must change. For during these years I had learnt much; I had come to know Hospital Assistants who were both courteous and helpful and I had no intention of accepting anything else from him. He grunted assent, typically. I thought over his attitude and decided that a part might stem from the conflicting status of white and black and that he, not unreasonably, might harbour resentment that though undoubtedly an able man, he was in an inferior position because of the colour of his skin.

One day he called me to see a man whom he had admitted with a diagnosis of a broken femur. I went to see the patient with him. The man was an African in his late thirties, lying on his back in bed with his leg partly bent and turned inwards, resting on his other leg, in obvious pain. I asked the Hospital Assistant how many fractured femurs had he seen before? 'Twenty . . . perhaps thirty.' (He had had about that number of years as a Hospital Assistant and had probably indeed seen about that number of such patients.) 'In what direction were their feet pointing?' I asked. Some thought, then (quite correctly): 'Outwards'. 'And this man's is pointing inwards. Therefore the diagnosis of fractured femur may not be correct. Feel gently along the upper end; it might be a dislocation and you may be able to feel the head of the femur lying behind the socket.' He felt as directed, except that he was not gentle. He appeared quite unaware of the pain to the patient and I remembered that his apparent unawareness had been characteristic of him in the past; he was not an unkind man but the patient as a sensitive being did not seem to exist for him. I took the patient's leg and gently manoeuvred it so that the head of the bone followed back along the course that it had taken when it was forced by the injury out of its socket. Arrived opposite the socket it popped in with a satisfying 'Pock'.

I said that the men who brought him in should not be allowed to go as they would be able to carry him home before evening and he need not spend the night in hospital. Having inflicted thus a minimum of injury to the Hospital Assistant's *amour propre,* I left him to think it over, as I knew he would. For the correction of the diagnosis had stemmed, not from my privileged position as a white but simply from observation of a situation of which he had had far more experience than I.

Some time later, I got a message from him asking me to come quickly, which I did — quickly. In the female ward lay a Bantu woman naked on a bed, with small splashes of water bedewing her; she was beautiful, but she was dead, as I quickly ascertained. I asked how it had occurred. It seemed she had been admitted with a very high temperature and the Hospital Assistant had sponged her down, whereupon she had collapsed and died. All this was recounted by the man without any attempt to excuse or defend himself (for which he deserved credit). I explained without recrimination that though indeed this was standard treatment in many textbooks, it was assumed that whoever administered it would be very well aware of his patient's condition by virtue of his experience and training, and would stop it at the first sign of ill effects.

Thenceforth he did, over the months, develop an increased awareness of his patients as living beings which was more in accord with his training and accomplishments. In the handling of a mass of clinical material it is not possible to anticipate every misadventure and at least in this case some benefit resulted.

I have earlier described how the patient was given his day's ration of drugs, told to count them and to keep them in his hand; the dresser would then tell him when he was due to swallow the next dose. Not only did I feel it degrading for the African dressers but unlikely to lead to cordial relations between my staff and me. Though Jan Morris in her Trilogy regrets the aloofness of whites from blacks it is very difficult to be on friendly terms (or indeed any reasonable sort of terms) with someone whom one needs to watch constantly for corruption. In the same sort of way we kept continual watch on the issue and use of anti-syphilitic drugs which commanded good prices on the black market, to stop empty ampoules beng used to prevent under-dosage from becoming apparent.

Eventually, however, in Cholo, my dressers began to 'think big' and an intact tin of a thousand sulphathiozole tablets disappeared. I traced it and the thief by the well-known method of 'information received'. A letter from an African employed on a near-by tea estate was left in one of the medical textbooks in my office where I was certain to find it. It was a charmingly written 'roofer' to one of my dressers and it ended on the note: 'By the way, could you let me have a further supply of that M & B?' That evening the premises of the addressee were searched by the police and the supply of M & B was found. Sent to prison the thief must have cudgelled his brains as to who had betrayed him and in due course I received 'further information' which enabled the police to recover a further supply of stolen goods and to put one further prisoner into gaol. The encounter between the two criminals might have been entertaining to overhear. It was something of a relief when the trail dried up for my staff was becoming somewhat depleted.

The catalogue of crime at this hospital ended on a mere allegation of misdemeanour; two dressers were alleged to have been 'flown' with drink and to have entered the women's ward and made advances to some of the inmates. On looking into this it seemed to be more appropriately a subject for a Fursean lecture, so I assembled the staff and pointed out that here we were, doing our best to prepare the people for eventual self-rule and what hopes had we when they behaved as they had recently been behaving? The staff listened with politely wooden faces, with the exception of one man whom I felt to be very honest, on whose face deep mortification was clear. Later privately he said: 'All the men knew what you were talking about. The trouble is that we have all of us done . . . things . . . and we all know this about each other. Even I have done . . . things . . . and the others know it.'

Experienced in Indian matters, Lord Hailey in his revised 'African Survey' wisely warns us that we must expect and accept a certain degree of corruption. In the days of which I am writing there was little, if any, corruption among public servants in England, but there is little doubt that it has been rampant at times in her history.

We were still at Cholo when United Kingdom leave was resumed at the end of the war in Europe and we were then sent on a year's back leave to England in August 1945. Having made up my mind not to return to Nyasaland, we travelled with all our personal possessions, packed in two heavy tin-lined trunks, three smaller tin trunks, a helmet case containing our topees and a 'Wolsey' helmet, (never worn and already old-fashioned), wooden boxes, suitcases (Including two heavy leather ones, of beautiful quality, a wedding present from my wife who had chosen them in London in 1939, 'in case I went to the war!') and three children, Robin (5), Tom (3) and Iris (15 months). Our paraffin refrigerator, bed linen, our few pictures and books, and the long mirror, followed us in about eighteen months time.

In Beira (Portuguese East Africa) and Bulawayo (Southern Rhodesia) we changed trains and were able to book into a hotel for a few hours in each place to wash off the grime of the train in comfort. After six days we arrived in Capetown. There were no porters so I unloaded our thirty-five pieces of luggage, helped by a carefree bachelor friend (how I envied him!) and we eventually found the hotel where we had made our booking for the three nights before the *SS Drottningholm* sailed. (Luggage-lifters-lumbago afflicted me for some time as a result of these activities.)

The ship was a Swedish 'mercy ship', manned by Swedes and (presumably) hired by the British Government to help to bring its nationals home once the war in Europe was over. She carried 250 RAF wives, whose husbands were to be demobbed later, their children, mostly under five, my wife and our children and six men. The latter were given the best cabins, with beds and a porthole, two men to each cabin. My wife and the children shared a cabin with two bunks and Iris slept in a carry-cot on the floor, the carpet of which housed some biting insect. A sky-light opened onto the deck above and when it was open, in the tropics, debris thrown by the passengers or their children collected on the top bunk. On deck we sat on the planks or on the hatches for there were no deck chairs and much time was spent queueing for the washing facilities and the one iron — drip dry clothes had yet to be invented. Nearing the Bay of Biscay the weather grew colder and in the Bay the sea became very rough; most of the women were sick and some lay on the hard deck, while their children crawled or scrambled over them. At times in Nyasaland we had had recourse to the slogan: 'Nothing lasts for ever' and we had frequently to remind ourselves of this on our three week journey in the *Drottningholm.*

Interestingly enough we heard few grumbles. I think this was because the young wives were so eager to reach 'Home'. They had been separated from their immediate families for some years and knew that, in many cases, these same families had had to endure far worse things during the war than the discomforts of life on board ship.

We were met in Liverpool by my brother, Jim, still in uniform. My brothers had come through the war unscathed, though both had landed in France shortly after D day and seen much fighting — Dick in the Army and Jim in the Marines. As we travelled together in the train to London, my wife was astonished to learn that officers travelled first class while 'other ranks' went third — after six years in Africa it seemed strange to her to differentiate between people of the same colour and speaking the same language. Tom, who vomited before we left the ship, bringing up what appeared to be a multitude of pale pink worms (which we were relieved to discover were only bits of plasticine previously swallowed) vomited again on the train. What a motley, worn and travel-stained crew we must have appeared to our respective families gathered to greet us in London after so long an absence! They had survived the London blitz and the later doodlebugs and the only one missing was my father, who had died of cancer in 1942, and my brother-in-law and his family, still in Jamaica with ICI.

For the next two months our long-suffering relations on both sides sheltered us and then my sister-in-law very generously offered us a house she had inherited at Cooden Beach in Sussex, to live in until we could find one of our own. Like all those immediately on the southern coast, 'Harleston', in Beaulieu Road, had been requisitioned by the Army in 1940, when Hitler's invasion was daily expected and my sister-in-law had had to remove all the furniture and fittings at very short notice and keep them in store for the duration of the war. The house had later suffered flying bomb damage when the wall of the lounge had been blown out. The gap was now covered by a tarpaulin, but the Army had moved out of the area, the beach had been cleared of mines, and the owners were allowed back to their properties.

We moved down to Cooden in the middle of December 1945 and one van-load of some of the furniture was delivered by the London firm responsible for storing it. The four men unloading it had only recently been demobbed and we found their candid comments on our supposed status as owners of this high quality furniture and kitchen equipment most embarrassing, especially when the aluminium saucepans emerged. Many households had sacrificed their saucepans in 1941, the darkest days of the war, to help to make aircraft, and the men obviously did not believe that we were not the original owners of this Aladdin's cave of pre-war goods, seemingly unpatriotically stashed away for the 'duration'.

We were the only people living in Beaulieu Road for a couple of months and we had the beach, only about 100 yards away, virtually to ourselves. Then, gradually, in the spring, the houses, all big ones standing in fairly large gardens, were re-occupied and a semblance of normality returned to the area. There were very few private cars on the roads, as both cars and petrol (except for business purposes and the armed forces) were almost unobtainable, but the public services were good: there were buses to Bexhill and along the coast to Hastings, and to Eastbourne in the opposite direction. The trains to London, too, were fairly reliable, considering the age of the rolling stock.

Setting up housekeeping in post-war England, still tightly rationed, was not easy and posed problems in unexpected ways, especially for those coming from abroad. For example, to buy the disinfectant 'Dettol' from a chemist it was necessary to give him an empty Dettol bottle in exchange. We had no empty bottle so shops refused to serve us, thinking that we were 'trying it on'. Eventually we found a chemist who believed our story of having come from overseas but it was a new and unpleasant experience to have our word doubted and to be regarded as 'fiddlers'. We encountered this attitude in other shops too where empty containers were required to be returned before goods were sold.

A different difficulty was caused by soap! Detergents did not then exist and soap, both of the household and toilet variety, was rationed. The few laundries which had survived the war refused to take on new customers so my wife washed the clothes and bed linen in the bath. As every housewife knows, or knew then, household soap, which was sold in bars, has a much longer life if cut up and thoroughly dried, and prudent, pre-war housewives always kept reserve stocks so that 'new' soap was never used. Our weekly ration of (new) soap, almost as soft as butter, melted away in the wash like snow in the sun. Luckily my wife's sister, who had begun the war with a large stock of dried-out soap, and was on the books of a laundry, generously gave us some of her precious store. Later in the year a laundry in Bexhill was able to take us on as customers, as its staff was demobilised and returned to work for it.

We were very lucky in two respects. I visited the appropriate authorities in Bexhill to obtain our ration of boiler fuel and to register with a coal merchant, and when it was revealed that we had come from the tropics and had three children under 5½, we were allowed an extra ration. There was a boiler in the kitchen and we made the kitchen our living room and so kept warm; luckily it was a fairly mild winter.

I also visited the Labour Exchange after Christmas and asked, with but little hope, if they had anyone on their books who would come and help in the house. To our amazement a young woman (Miss Edna Russell of blessed memory) appeared the next day. She had just been demobbed, had returned to her family in Bexhill and was wanting domestic work. She was a very hard worker, always cheerful, and when snow stopped the buses, she walked the two miles from Bexhill. She remained with us all the time we spent in 'Harleston' and, when I began work in London in the New Year, she was always willing to look after the children while my wife queued for the rations in Bexhill, and, later in the year, for bread coupons when bread was also rationed.

I have described two of the pinpricks and our two lucky breaks. Overall, however, was the much greater anxiety that we had to find a house of our own before I left England again. In pre-war days the school-age children of Colonial servants in the tropics were frequently left with relations or friends in the United Kingdom, but post-war conditions made this impossible. During the war, many children on the outstations in Nyasaland began their education with a correspondence course and then, later, travelled down to Southern Rhodesia or South Africa for their schooling. As I was hoping for a transfer to some other colony (and this might not necessarily be in Africa) and as we wanted our children to be brought up in a healthy climate and to have an English education, my wife and I had decided that for a few years at least, we must run two households and that the childrens' needs should be paramount. It was a decision all Colonial servants faced in those far-off days. The aeroplane, by which children could be flown out for school holidays, eventually changed all that but in 1946, this, if it ever crossed our minds, we dismissed as a pipe dream.

We hoped to buy a three-bedroomed house, four-bedroomed if possible, within reach of buses, shops and schools. It was reckoned that one paid £1000 a bedroom. My wife had no capital and mine at that time consisted of £2650 from a half-share in one of my father's far sighted investments — Kentwater Cottage at Cowden, in Kent — and about £500 from a lucky investment of £100 before the war. Because of the scarcity due to war damage, houses were snapped up almost before they came on the market and no property was surveyed before purchase, for fear of losing it to some other eager buyer. We had seen a few unsuitable, dilapidated houses in isolated villages before moving to Cooden Beach; the only one which seemed at all suitable to my wife cost £4500 and I refused even to go and see it. My financial position in the future with a house to buy and furnish, two households to maintain and future school bills, was beginning to cause me much concern. We went round houses in Bexhill, Cooden and Little Common, (having no car limited our range), but they were all in the price range of £4000 and upwards, anything less was either much too small or verging on slum property.

In the spring and growing desperate we contemplated building, as my mother had told us of building plots available at Tekels Park, the headquarters of the Theosophical Society at Camberley. There was very little land for building on the market as building permission was difficult to obtain. Moreover there was a restriction on the size of house, only small houses costing up to a certain limit were permitted; I believe the limit was in the region of £1250. The plot at Tekels was expensive — £400 — but we asked a young architect living there to design us a house and apply for building permission. To cut a long story short we then found the price of the land had to be included in the £1250 and abandoned the plan.

It was by then the early autumn of 1946, so my wife's sister resumed the search in her vicinity on our behalf and that of their brother, who was by then also in the United Kingdom and houseless. One day we received a telephone call: 'Come up here immediately. I've seen a house in Reigate I think will do and have asked the people to give you first refusal'. My wife obeyed post-haste, looked over the house the next day and had to decide then and there whether to buy it. The owner was asking £3750 and refused to bring the price down; £3500 had been our limit as we had to furnish it. Unable to consult me she decided it was the most suitable house we had yet seen and plunged.

No. 4, Smoke Lane, Reigate, was small but very well built; Mr Hodge, the builder, in fact, lived next door. It was situated on high ground on the southern edge of Reigate, close to the open fields leading to South Park, then a small development on the perimeter, but near shops and comparatively close to schools and the station. The town itself was still a pleasant market town, set in the pretty Surrey countryside between two folds of the North Downs. The old charcoal-burners' path (the origin of the name Smoke Lane), shaded by trees, led from the end house down the hill, past a sand and gravel pit on the right, to the main road. Here the Reigate-East Grinstead buses passed every half-hour, stopping in the village of Copthorne, nearly

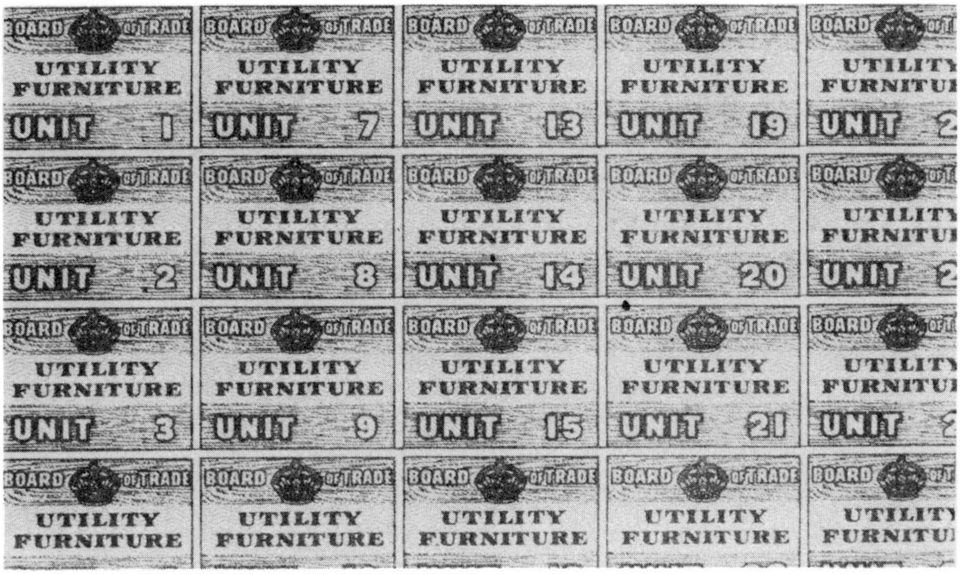

Board of Trade Utility Furniture Buying Permit

To be quoted in any correspondence
Reference Number N 4985460
Name of holder Mrs V. A. Berry

National Registration Identity Card Number or Service Number and Rank

Address

Date of Issue 7 Jan 1947

Area of Validity
This permit may be used ONLY at a shop within a radius of 15 miles of the address to which the furniture is to be delivered or anywhere in UF 8 193099
XXX

1. You cannot use this permit until a date which will be announced later by the Board of Trade. Take great care of it and watch the newspapers for the announcement which will tell you when you can use it and for how long it will be valid.

2. The name of the person to whom this permit was issued is entered on the front and the permit may only be used by or on behalf of that person. He should fill in his address before using the permit.

3. When shopping you must hand the complete permit to the shopkeeper. If there are more units than he needs for your order he will cut out the number required and return the rest to you. You must not cut units out yourself and it is illegal for the shopkeeper to accept loose units.

4. The shopkeeper may not retain units except when an order has been placed.

5. When ordering goods by post send the complete permit with your order. The shopkeeper will return the units he does not need.

6. This permit which is the property of H.M. Government may be used ONLY by or on behalf of the person to whom it is issued and ONLY within the area of validity shown overleaf.

outside the house where lived my wife's sister and her family and very close to her parents, who had moved to Copthorne after the blitz on London.

The house had a sitting room, facing north and very cold, with an open fireplace and with French windows leading into a very small garden; a south-facing dining-room, which became the children's playroom, heated by a gas fire, and a kitchen looking out onto a passage and fence which divided us from the next house. A small boiler, burning anthracite, warmed the kitchen and provided hot water in the winter; during the summer, gas water heaters over the sink and bath were used. At this period one was still adjured not to bath in more than five inches of water; my wife having lived in places where the water supply was sometimes deficient in the dry season and muddy in the wet, found five inches of clean water almost luxurious. Upstairs, the main bedroom and a small dressing room faced south; two smaller bedrooms were on the north side with a distant prospect over Reigate of Colley Hill and the Downs to the north of the town; a bathroom faced west over the kitchen. The bedrooms were unheated and there was no garage, nor was there space for one.

Like most of our generation we had both been brought up to believe that one did without things unless one could pay for them, so my wife was very shaken when Jim, in charge of our legal arrangements, suggested that he should arrange a small private mortgage for us. In my wife's family a mortgage was unheard of and only people with dubious finances indulged in them! (The days when young couples began married life with a Building Society mortgage as a matter of course were still very much in the future.)

We could not, in fact, have managed without the mortgage for furnishing the house proved very expensive. A certain amount of basic 'Utility' furniture was made available by the Government on coupons — this was to help families who had been bombed out or, like us, were setting up homes for the first time. It was well designed, well made, reasonable in price but uniform, like the 'Utility' clothes we all wore and which were also only available on coupons. We bought very sparingly beginning with five metal beds and mattresses, 'off the ration' and not very comfortable. We had brought sheets from Nyasaland and a few thin blankets, quite

Vouchers for Clothing Coupons 1946

inadequate for an English winter. Shops would only supply one blanket per customer, so we asked our relations each to buy a blanket and pass it on to us. Even my wife's hairdresser in Bexhill bought one in her lunch hour when she heard of our straits. The owner of the house sold us (at a price!) the sitting room carpet, together with the hall, landing and stair carpet, the kitchen table and four chairs. Curtain material was unobtainable, but Northovers of Reigate supplied us with curtains made of hessian (i.e. sacking) dyed green. The bedroom floors, fortunately, were already covered in linoleum and so was the kitchen. My parents-in-law had lent a chest-of-drawers to a friend during the war and this came to us, together with a desk from my wife's old home — the only elegant piece of furniture we possessed.

The paraffin refrigerator (and the long mirror) arrived a few weeks later. (The former was already ten years old and had travelled with me from house to house in Nyasaland. Sometimes it failed to make ice. Then it was laid on its front (without the lamp), thumped heartily on its back and set on its legs again — cured. My wife had it converted to electricity and it functioned (unserviced) for another *twenty-five years!*)

We moved from Cooden Beach to Reigate in January, 1947. One of our relations, secure in a house bought before the war and very adequately furnished with nothing but the best, referred to it as our 'poky little house' — little realising the happiness it brought to my wife to feel settled at last in a home of our own, however small and sparsely furnished, after the first seven peripatetic years of our married life, and though we both faced a future of long separations in the course of my work.

Chapter 7

As soon as we arrived in England, late in 1945, I had contacted Platt to report on our failures in the Nutrition Unit, to put forward some conclusions and to suggest a way of putting these conclusions into practice.

During the war Platt's career had gone from strength to strength in the national and international field of nutrition. He served as joint secretary of the Scientific Food Policy Committee of the War Cabinet from 1940-45 and was a member of the Committee on Medical and Nutritional Aspects of Food Policy (COMA). In 1943 he went to the Hot Springs Conference in America (devoted to ensuring adequate supplies of food for all in the future) and in 1944 became Director of the Medical Research Council's Human Nutrition research unit. He visited the British West Indies to initiate research (where he insisted that the spearhead of attack on malnutrition must be medical), and attended the United Nations Food and Agriculture Organisation conference at Quebec. In 1945 he was awarded a CMG. During my year in England in 1946 he was appointed honorary head of the newly formed Department of Human Nutrition at the London School of Hygiene and Tropical Medicine and was given the title of Professor of Human Nutrition by the University of London.

I had returned from Nyasaland convinced by then of two things. The first was that, because he suffered from under nutrition rather than malnutrition, a full belly was of more importance to the African villager than a great variety of new subsidiary foods. The bottle-neck which prevented him from growing more food was the very short time at the beginning of the rains when land could be cleared using a hoe as the only tool. Not only did this restrict the amount of land which could be cleared but the clearing had to be done during the 'hungry season' when his food supply was low. From the dietary records carried out on the Bantu in the Nyasaland Nutrition Survey, Platt had been able to prepare running estimates of energy expenditure to compare with energy intakes, (a completely new approach to us at the time).

Discussing this energy deficit which, together with the time factor, were limiting influences in agricultural activity, I expressed my belief that any major improvement in African nutrition would have to involve the introduction of mechanised agriculture, as the presence of tsetse fly made the introduction of draught cattle very hazardous. A bold experiment was needed to try to introduce it on a *very small scale,* with the full cooperation of the villagers and their chief, explaining each step fully to them before putting it into practice.

The second point on which I was convinced was that the system of Indirect Rule — or rather of Direct Rule masked as Indirect — was destroying the tribal structure rather than upholding it. I felt very strongly that any policy to grow more food *must* be done with the willing cooperation of the Chiefs, as *leaders of their people,* and not imposed from above, and that responsibility for the success or failure of a scheme should be shouldered by the people.

I elaborated on this later in a paper I read to a meeting, called in Oxford in 1946 by Major Ralph Furse, to an invited audience of selected District Commissioners to voice their perturbations about the future of Empire. (Mr Creech Jones was then Secretary of State for the Colonies). In it I made quite clear my view that the 'young men' — the first generation of western-educated Africans — were getting very restive. To them indirect rule stood for an alliance made between imperial and tribal authority to restrain their own advance. I suggested that they should be encouraged to take on responsibility, in the first place, of rural dispensaries, such as we had in

Nyasaland. These should be run by local funds drawn either on the lines of a cooperative society or on a local authority basis, much like the rates in England. The object being that there should be a clear relationship in the native mind between local tax paid out and benefits received locally. (This conclusion I had reached as a result of the incident of theft of Sulphathiazole described in the previous chapter.)

After discussion, Platt offered me a post in his organisation, which I accepted, and in the New Year he negotiated my temporary transfer from the Colonial Service. I then went up to London daily, either to the London School of Tropical Medicine or the Colonial Office, spending some six hours a day travelling. I caught the 6.20 a.m. train from Cooden Beach, arriving back about 8.0 p.m. on weekdays and 3.30 p.m. on Saturdays.

Platt advised me to go through the Annual Reports of various colonies in search of instances where mechanised agriculture had been considered or where mechanisation had been or was being tried out. Of many such reports which I then read the only territory which sounded promising was the tiny West African colony and Protectorate of Gambia. Here small scale trials were reported using a tractor and second-hand ploughs and implements on the alluvial rice-growing swamps on either side of the river Gambia, which ran salt for a variable distance and was navigable to ocean-going steamers for 150 miles. The alluvial land on either side of the river amounted to an estimated 250,000 acres.

A proposal was therefore put up to the Colonial Office for a *Nutrition Field Working Party,* comprising initially a medical officer (myself), a dietician cum economist, an agronomist and an all-purpose administrator. These were to work under Platt's aegis in Gambia, to make a preliminary Survey and then to grow rice or other crops, using machinery which the Agricultural Department considered suitable. Later a mechanic was added to the list.

Platt introduced me to John Wakefield, the ex-Director of Agriculture, Tanganyika, who was interested in our project, and who in that year, 1946, spent three months investigating the possibility of a scheme for growing large quantities of groundnuts in Tanganyika. He advised us on what machinery we should need for bush clearance, etc. In the post-war period complex machines were almost unobtainable, but I interviewed, on Platt's behalf, an official of Ford's of Dagenham, with the result that we were almost the only team in the field of Colonial development to have at our disposal a new Fordson Major tractor. Besides Platt's natural gifts, he had the backing of power and money. His approach was to find the man, or machine, and then to negotiate within the Colonial Office to find the money, where others, less daring, waited on the money and so lost the opportunity to obtain the man — or machine.

The cooperation of the Gambian Agricultural Department was asked for and in July 1946 I flew out to Bathurst (now Banjul) for a preliminary reconnaissance and discussions, in the company of a soil chemist, Hugh Bunting, of Platt's Department, who later played an important part in the ill-fated Tanganyika Groundnut Scheme.

We were welcomed by the Administrative Officers but informed that the Gambia had been severely drained of resources during the war. (From the fall of France in 1940, until Germany's surrender in 1945, she had been wedged between territories of 'Vichy' France, also, her supplies of rice from the Far East had been cut off when the Japanese entered the war in 1942.) They would help all they could but they were short of staff and supplies and, for the most part, whatever we wanted to do would need to be done by ourselves. Cars were scarce, lorries almost unobtainable, the Colony's store of all nails much reduced by the incursions of someone, who, thinking bigger than my thief of sulphathiazole in Nyasaland, had sawn through the store padlock and then replaced it, so that the cut was not noticed, and helped himself to nine tons of nails. Also if we wished to house our European staff upcountry, which we obviously would wish, *we* must build their houses for them.

This said, I would like to add that in the process of establishing a toe-hold where we ultimately decided was suitable, I found the Government staff very cooperative and helpful, though all working under great difficulties created by the post-war conditions and shortages.

The country, round the small colony of Bathurst and Kombo St. Mary on the coast, was reminiscent of the flat lands with palm trees outside Fort Johnston in Nyasaland, but with a pleasant breezy cliff leading down to the Atlantic. We had an interview with the Governor (Sir Hilary Blood) and, in a car provided by Gambia Government, we toured the alluvial land of the Protectorate beyond the Colony, mainly on the south side of the River Gambia. The river flows from east to west into the Atlantic and the Protectorate occupied a narrow strip of land some ten miles wide on either side. Mangrove swamps fringed the banks of the river and an earth road ran parallel to it on the south side. Villages, consisting of huts, each with its own 'yard', surrounded by a *'krinting'* (woven bamboo) fence, were scattered at intervals in the flat landscape of the bush. I wrote to my wife: 'On the soil side, there are, it seems, plenty of problems . . .'

The reality of the soil problems was illustrated by experience in Sierra Leone, as I discovered when I visited it later in the year on my way back from a conference at Kumasi in Gold Coast (now Ghana). The effect of bunding off land there — to keep out river water which ran salt seasonally each year and so hampered rice production — had, in the agricultural officers' experience, proved lethal, not only to planted rice but also to weeds naturally present and even to rice on the borders of poldered land.[(1)] In Freetown I met the Director of Agriculture and I wrote home:

> '. . . he is worried because he does not think his department can go at the pace that he thinks we want to set. I reassured him a bit. Actually I am anxious to

Gambia — village street with 'krinting' fences surrounding 'yards'

> slow down the pace as much as I can too. Hugh Bunting and Platt have not the remotest idea of the difficulties before us. I want to get a chit from the D. of A. to the effect that he thinks the first year (after the Survey) should be spent in trials of types of machinery . . . and not in costings . . .'

I was to go out in January 1947 (Platt being confident that the Colonial Office would approve the vote) in order to build the houses in which we were to live, the rest of the team to follow in April, after the vote was approved.

I was anxious that a young man named Carter should be engaged as early as possible as the agronomist to the team. He had worked on the alluvial lands at the mouth of the River Severn in England, but though he had been interviewed early in July, nothing definite had as yet been fixed. In the event he decided he could wait no longer and Platt then engaged a woman agronomist and a woman dietician. The male administrator had been in the Army and was interested in West African languages. He was only finally engaged when I had already been some months in Gambia and I had not previously met him.[(2)]

The first year was to be spent on a *Survey* and the next two into *Research into Development* — i.e. into the introduction of farm mechanisation into a rural economy, and I was required to make a six monthly progress report to the Hailey Research Committee.

The Survey was to consist of:

1. A clinical and physical examination of a limited sample in the chosen village and spot samples in other villages, and to calculate energy expenditure of men, women and children in these samples. (My work, with help from the dietician).
2. To record and weigh what the people in the samples ate and sociological data about them. (The dietician's work).
3. To estimate the acreage and record all crops the people were cultivating. (The agronomist's work).

We argued that if we kept serial weighings, we would know when the energy output of the villagers exceeded their intake. From our records of the amount of time spent in various sorts of tasks — to prepare the land, later to sow, weed, protect from pests and finally harvest — we would know what were the most arduous tasks in terms of energy expenditure and when they were incurred. Where the precise form of work of our farmers had not been measured by calorimetry and reported, we would make use of Platt's technique of comparing the task with certain known activities.

Hugh Bunting and I had decided on the village of Genieri and the region roundabout it as suitable for the Survey and for development of the swamp lands, rather than Yoroberikunda, further up-river, where one of Platt's nutritionists[(3)] was doing a pilot nutrition survey. The *phragmites* reed flourishes where the water runs sweet as it did for long periods at 'YBK'; where the flow is salt the reed growth is checked and so makes clearance easier. At Genieri, the river ran salt for a sufficiently long period in the year to check the reed growth, but in the rains when the river flooded, this flood water in due course ran sweet. The villagers carried out a simple but practical test in which they transplanted rice seedlings in advance of these floods. If the river was still too salt the seedlings died, but if they lived this was the signal for tremendous activity and planting out of seedlings, which had been nurtured on sweet water from wells. It was largely a womens' crop and very hard work.

Later, during our Survey, we heard of one woman (and one only), who consistently over previous years had practised selection of seed from what appeared to be the most promising rice plants. She gained a certain local fame and had a ready sale for such seed as she judged she could spare. It was in contrast to the clever men whom I described in Nyasaland as being 'like good deeds in a naughty world', in that, as far as we knew, her success bred no resentment among her fellows.

I left my family in January 1947, a week after we moved to Reigate and a week before the coldest winter for years gripped the country and covered it in ice and snow for six weeks. In the heat of the Gambia it was difficult for me to visualize the conditions in which my wife was living, for the children were ill, the heating was inadequate, the water pipes froze (and then burst in the thaw), and electricity black-outs were frequent. The latter occurred when workers returned in the evening from 5.0 p.m. onwards, and switched on lights, fires and cookers, and the resultant 'surge' overloaded the country's ageing electrical system. The authorities, urging their cold consumers to economise, tried to distribute the black-outs fairly, district by district, but it was never possible to know in advance when one's turn would come and the cuts lasted from half to one and a half hours (and sometimes longer if there was an actual breakdown). By late February I was determined that she should, if possible, come out to the Gambia for part of the next winter and my letters over the next few months contain frequent references as to how we were to achieve this. It was still very difficult to get air passages for non-official passengers and each traveller was allowed to take only £5 sterling out of the country, an amount inadequate to cover subsistence in a foreign country if the planes were delayed *en route* as sometimes happened.

Platt and I flew out to Bathurst together and up by lorry to the rest house at Kaiaff, a few miles away from Genieri, where we were to plan the headquarters for the Survey. The road was as bad as, and in places, worse than the Nyasaland earth roads; it was not an all-weather road and was sometimes impassable in the rainy season due to floods. We sat in deck chairs in the back of the lorry and going over one of the many bumps my deck chair and I rose so far from the lorry that when I landed again one of the legs of the chair was broken and the metal cross piece bent!

Platt wanted three villages surveyed, in a similar way to the Nyasaland Survey, but we soon discovered that the differences between the Gambian villages were not as marked as they had been in the Nyasaland hill, foothill and Lakeshore areas. He also agreed that it was better to do a group of 3-400 people and others as spot samples, instead of the group of 1000 which had been originally planned. I pointed out to him from the start that we would need to introduce mechanisation into the community very slowly and carefully so as to carry the villagers with us and that it would be fatal to our scheme if we tried to go too far, too fast, especially with untried machinery. Furthermore, if, because of 'soil problems' rice cultivation proved unpromising we would have to shift from rice to ground nuts. This was the major cash crop of the Gambia and so should enable the African indirectly to fill his belly until the 'problems' had been sorted out.

After a day spent choosing a site for the Survey houses on higher ground, to catch any breeze and a fair distance from the swamp, and meeting the *Seyfu* (Chief), we travelled back over the bumps. Platt gave a statesmanlike review of the position to the Gambian Heads of Department and, for the medical research side of the project which he proposed to set up at Fajara, outside Bathurst, he was able to obtain the use of the German ex-Lufthansa house — a big house on the seashore, beautifully cool and with lovely bathing.

My task during the next four months was to build, at Genieri, three European-type houses, a dispensary, store houses, and African staff houses; to set up a 'hospital' (like my medical camps in Nyasaland) and, by living among them, to get to know the people. I had never built a house before, so Platt arranged for a master builder attached to his Unit at Mill Hill, to come out to Gambia for three weeks to initiate me into the rudiments of house building.

On my return to Genieri by the river steamer, and while awaiting him, I began, with the cooperation of the *Seyfu,* to get the sundried bricks made and to collect the mangrove poles we would need for the roof. I had brought up the cement for the floors from Bathurst on the steamer, but the Public Utility Works (PUD) were unable to supply us with window frames as they only had enough for their own requirements.

The houses were to be of the simplest — one bedroom, one living room and, if possible, a bathroom, all mosquito proofed. One of my main preoccupations was to make them cool, for the temperature rose to 115° and more in the dry season, and weatherproof. Unless the grass thatch was firmly secured the high winds experienced at certain seasons would whip it off. The thatch had also to withstand the tropical rainstorms. In the meantime I planned to live in the rest house at Kaiaff, surrounded by my loads, with a table made of two boxes and another box to sit on. Our 'vote' was not yet through and I feared to spend money on furniture in case I did not see it back. The vote went through, but from the 1st March 1947. I heard later that when the money was being voted by the Colonial Office, it was hotly opposed by the Treasury, but Mr Creech Jones, the Secretary of State for the Colonies, knew a great deal about Colonial affairs. He had also been in the audience at the Oxford meeting when I read my paper on dispensaries, mentioned earlier. The money would have been vetoed had he not been able, as I wrote to my wife: 'to shove his oar in' and the vote went through, but for three years only. While waiting, I borrowed a Tilley petrol lamp and wrote urgently to my wife to send our Nyasaland lamps out with

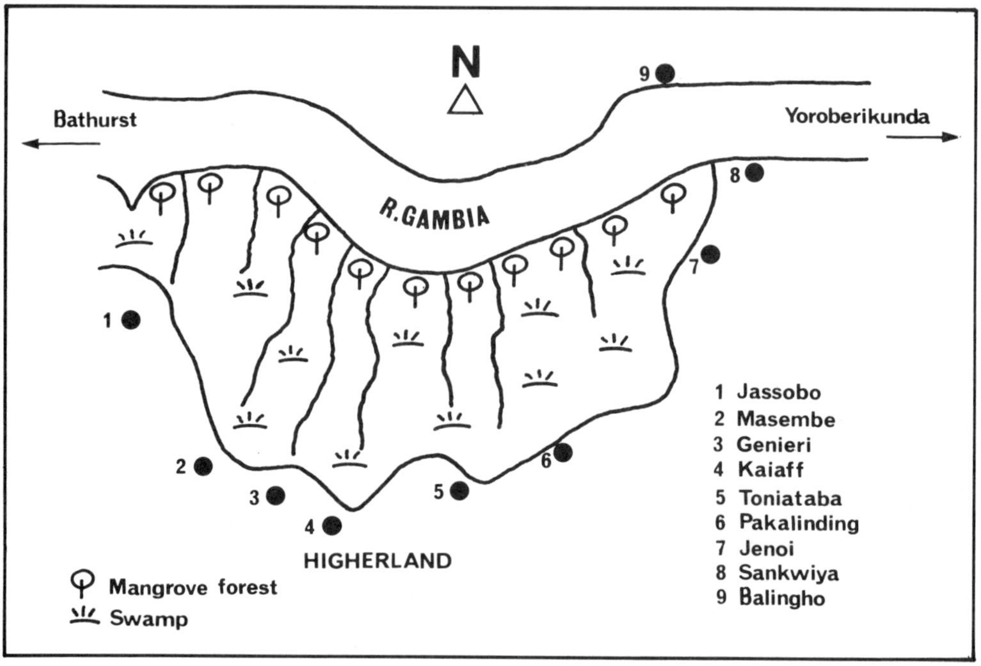

From a letter dated 1.2.47
"Rough idea of the lay-out. An Immense stretch of swamp about 5 miles long and a mile deep . . ."

spare mantles, if she could obtain them. I had no transport yet so either walked or depended on lifts from lorries transporting ground nuts to the river wharf.

Besides the two tons of cement and a load of tools for building, I had brought up my medical kit, bedding, crockery and food from Bathurst on the river steamer. Fellow passengers were six MPs out from England, two Conservatives and four Labour members. They were all interested in what we were proposing to do and a Labour MP, James Callaghan, said, in parting, that they would be watching out for the results of our experiment. Unfortunately I was then engaged in counting the bags of cement being unloaded, for unless such deliveries were checked, they were apt to be landed one or two short, and having reached the thirties of my count, I was loth to break off and bid him goodbye with the courtesy I would have liked. In due course he became Prime Minister of the United Kingdom.

I began my medical work immediately, in the dispensary at Kaiaff, and soon had a steady trickle of patients with malaria, minor accidents and a child with suspected cerebrospinal fever. The father of the sick child offered me an egg — he was obviously very poor, but I refused it saying that I could not take rewards for my work. I took a number of blood samples to try out the method of counting parasites by mixing the blood with an equal volume of a suspension of fowl cells, though it took me some time to master the technique, and each day I tried to add about fifteen new words in Mandinka to my vocabulary.

The master builder (nicknamed 'Pop') arrived on the 7th February and by the 12th the foundations of the main room and the second room of my house had been laid, but progress was painfully slow. I then remembered from my Nyasaland days two planters, whose methods of dealing with labour were very different. One, lean and irascible, spent his days perpetually urging his labour force to further effort and more conscientious performance. In this he suffered from a clash of interest with his men whose object in life was to do the minimum of work and in the easiest way; and to try to ascertain by dint of experience the point at which their employer's tolerance became exhausted.

The other man spent a considerable time working out the time which various tasks should take. He defined for his men's benefit certain tasks, the completion of which constituted a fair day's work; at the beginning of the day these tasks were set out, and any objections had to be stated. Otherwise his supervision was largely limited to inspection made at frequent intervals while there was still time to point out poor workmanship and to rectify it. Characteristically this man spent his day unruffled.

The Gambian concept of the maximum day's work was outrageously low in comparison with the Bantu of Nyasaland. 'We shall never get the houses built before the girls arrive.' said Pop gloomily, watching the long line of men and boys trailing reluctantly with blocks of sun-dried clay from the grey soil at the edge of the swamp to the site we had chosen. By that time I had watched them for long enough to be able to define a fair day's work in terms of blocks carried, and I therefore told the lackadaisical crew that after they had deposited a stated number of blocks they could knock off work. At once they were galvanised into activity; even the smallest and slightest of them came staggering up the slope, their trunks bending under the load, so that I feared lest they might do themselves an injury. Far earlier than we had expected, the task was done and Pop and I returned to Kaiaff well satisfied with the prospects for future building.

For more intricate work such as brick laying, I found that if I worked alongside the men myself, sharing stint and stint alike, this again kept the pace of work going. There was, however, a snag. We had chosen a site near a huge cotton tree the home of a swarm of bees, and these unfortunately proved to be *racist* bees. They would pick their way down the labour gang in a perfunctory manner until they came to me, when they would attack me with peculiar vindictiveness. In the dusk, too, when I later sat sipping a well-earned sundowner, the home-coming bees would blunder at a great rate into the glass of my lamp, after which, infuriated, would look around for a scapegoat. And, guided no doubt by my differing smell, would invariably find and sting me.

When the house walls were well raised and we were tidying up, one of the labourers, referring to our early experience of one another, said: 'When we first knew you, we thought you were a very particular man and most difficult to please.' The absence of the least sign of self-criticism amused me!

Pop, however, was an instant success with the labourers. He had no teeth of his own and his way of evincing surprise at whatever he was told, was to open his mouth very wide in simulated astonishment, whereon his upper denture fell with a clatter onto his lower one. This so intrigued the labour gang that they would come to him with quite fictitious messages calculated to provoke Pop's standard reaction. He invariably obliged to their delight.

Having adapted our approach in the light of my recollections of the Nyasaland planters, we presented every kind of work in the form of finite piecework, which the Gambians did quickly and, so long as we kept an eye on them, well. Without piecework, individuals had to be incessantly goaded, the work took far longer and was done grudgingly and slowly. We soon decided we must do without the store-room/bathroom extension and to have the bath in the bedroom and a store fitting in one corner of the bedroom. The girls' houses were to be back to back and I wrote home: 'We can all have breakfast and lunch on my open place and have our suppers separately. Suppertime is the time when tempers are most likely to be frayed . . .' (In the event we all ate together for each meal.)

In the intervals of my medical work, of learning the art of building from Pop, and ordering vast quantitites of thatching grass, mud blocks and mangrove poles from roundabout, I began mapping the village and working out the family relationships of the inhabitants of the various 'yards' or compounds. But we were held up once more by the labour for all the men wished to be masons and none then wanted to carry bricks and water. The output of work temporarily doubled when I offered them £5 if they would finish in a week but tailed off again as I reported to my wife:

> '18.2.47 or is it the 19th? I'm not quite sure. I know I have missed one day but it may be two. I was very tired last night. The walls of the house were up to 8½ feet and the damned masons hadn't the guts to straddle the wall to lay bricks. So I went up and *stood* on it, its one foot thick! so there wasn't much chance of any sober person falling from it, and laid the bricks myself. Ultimately they realised what fools they were and settled down to the job properly. However I kept on, because progress is slow again and I can do it (a) quicker and (b) much less slapdashly than they do.'

Pop left two days later and I accompanied him to Bathurst. John Wakefield's advice in England had included the use of a giant tractor, a D 7, and one of my tasks was to make plans, well in advance, with the Agricultural Department in Bathurst, to off-load it from the ship and get it up to Genieri when it arrived. Bathurst possessed no crane capable of lifting it and there were few bridges across the many creeks that ran into the river between the port and our site at Genieri, strong enough to take its weight (11 tons).

One imaginative plan suggested was to off-load it from the ship at Bathurst onto a lighter, take it up river, cut the side of the lighter out and drive the tractor up the bank on a concrete ramp made for the job. The total cost would be £1000. Then it occurred to someone to enquire about some tank landing craft which had been

Gambia — The 'White Elephant'. D 7 tractor
with W. T. C. B., Tom and Iris

ordered by the Gambia Government the year before but had never arrived. It turned out that the Crown Agents had notified the Government that they were available in July 1946 and their letter had been pigeonholed ever since. So the Government cabled instructions home to send out the tractor and a tank landing craft in the same ship. They were at different ports, one in the north and one in the south of the UK, so it was arranged that after picking up the tractor the ship was to sail to the other port to pick up the landing craft.

Two days of stomach trouble, the discussions about the tractor and the difficulties involved in buying a lorry delayed me in Bathurst. There was a two-year delivery date quoted for new British lorries, so I bought a three ton clanking old Juggernaut. I picked up the driver through the Labour Officer in Bathurst when I had a good deal to learn about lorries. So had the laughing black policeman, controlling the traffic from a broad-based wooden shelter, which, not being used to driving with double tyres, I whisked away from under him as I turned into the main street. Half-way down my Juggernaut stalled. A friendly and vociferous crowd watched as the cook and I vainly wound the starting handle but our combined strength was barely enough to turn her over. Then I spotted my driver in the street and told him if he couldn't start it he was no driver for me. So he squared his shoulders and the lorry heaved and shook and started. His name was (ex-serjeant) Momadou and he had a reckless, resolute air which I liked.

I also bought a second-hand paraffin refrigerator, no new ones being available. This turned out to keep food cool but not cold and was always unsatisfactory. The following morning, laden to the brim with heavy equipment, Momadou, the cook and I drove back to Genieri along the grim road to Kaiaff, arriving in the night with a broken spring which was bound with ox-hide the next day. Later I played a game with the road, dusty and pot-holed in dry weather. If the lorry found an unexpected pothole and threw me upwards with sufficient force to strike my head on the roof of the lorry, that was one up to the road. If I remembered the particular pothole and circumnavigated it, that was one up to me. The road was much used by lorries driven by Africans, descendants of Jehu, but with a remarkable flair for keeping their ancient vehicles going, despite years of overloading. Momadou, a few days later, tightened a tappet, a thing I would never have dared to do and thereafter Juggernaut only had 99 knocks.

During my absence the building had not gone too badly but, as I informed my wife, the carpenters

> 'had rodgered the roof trusses, and I either had to use what they'd done or wait two days for more mangrove poles. So I used what they'd done and the roof is rather pec(uliar). Then we put in ceilings of woven bamboo splits onto which we will plaster mud later and then whitewash. We found we could not get one bit of ceiling through the door and had a pretty job getting it through the roof. The roof appears to hold together by force of gravity only . . .'

The house was thatched the next day and then the ceiling was mudded and a thin coat of cement washed over it when dry. All that then remained was to put in mosquito gauze and whitewash the house inside, but before that, on the 5th March, I saw from Genieri a column of black smoke arising from the Kaiaff direction. I drove the lorry there to find the rest house ablaze. A fire had started at one end of the village and swept up one side from thatched roof to roof taking the rest house on the way. The people had done great work in getting my stuff out (including three 60 gallon drums of petrol) and I lost nothing except my razor blades, but about 60-70 people were both homeless and foodless, their grainstores having been destroyed. Their many relations helped them with food and I promised the lorry to transport poles and grass from the swamp. But there was much gloom among the unfortunates and I spent the evening treating people with small burns.

I also had a pneumonia patient who was very ill and a child with an undiagnosable belly:

> 'I may have to explore under local (anaesthetic) . . .' I told my wife, 'as my total outfit here is one knife, two artery forceps, and a pair of blunt scissors, I am not looking forward to it. Now I am (perforce) in my own house. It is not finished, and the floor is deep in mud, grass, and cement, but it is clearly going to be a nice cool house.' The next day the house was finished: '. . . very sloppily, but sooner than have about a hundred men spitting all over the floor and staring in at the windows, for yet another day, I let them go and will get one good craftsman in later.'

The day before the fire at Kaiaff the elders of the village came to pay a formal call. Thinking that there would be about half a dozen in all, for I had been warned of the custom, I told the cook to prepare tea, but thirty arrived and I hardly dared look at my sugar supply afterwards, for we were rationed to 3 lbs per month, and they had enjoyed their tea.

Early in March I laid the foundations of the girls' house. Being now more experienced I picked out seven men from the vast horde of idlers that built my house and offered them a fixed sum to complete the building. The mason, a somewhat slapdash know-all, wanted more money than the others for being a mason but I told him that if he was not satisfied he could go, for I had to check up on every single course of bricks he laid. The seven good men and true and I worked hard at the new house all one day. It was a treat to have *workers* and to have bricks, mud and water on the site previously transported by Juggernaut. The carpenter made window frames for my house; they were accurate and upright and showed up the walls that the men had built while I was in Bathurst. One was about 8 inches out and it needed a great deal of cement and whitewash to cover the error.

Juggernaut, amidst bangs and rattles and a maximum turning lock of only 15 degrees, owing to the broken spring, was doing quite indispensable work collecting grass, poles, bricks, and three baths, wood and cement which had been dropped off at Sankwiya by the steamer; we would never have finished the houses without it. Some idea of the urgency of the task appears in the laconic record in a letter home: 'Lanced the driver's arse today' for Momadou had a boil, but remained master of Juggernaut in spite of all.

While we were hauling earth to fill in the foundations of the new house, I had my first visitors: the Bishop of Gambia, a female missionary and a young Dane, collecting monkeys for the Copenhagen Zoo. As the resthouse in Kaiaff was no more, they dossed down in some of my many little round houses. I presented a very pretty sight. My razor blades having been lost in the fire, I had a two-day growth of beard and I was inconceivably filthy.

On my next trip to Bathurst I was able to buy a small motor launch for river work and for use during the rains, (May/June to November), when the road was impassable, and my houseboy and I set out at 1.0 p.m. on the incoming tide for Genieri. About 9.30 p.m. with eight or nine miles to go, the gland nut holding the propellor shaft in place came loose and water began pouring in. Working in the dark with my hands under water, I repacked it with rag, by which time we were so full of water that we had to pull up the floor boards and bale hard. I anchored in mid-stream and we spent an uncomfortable night until dawn, when, starting her with much difficulty, we set out again. Unable to locate the *'bolon'* or creek leading to Genieri, among the many other creeks, I had to go across the river (where it is still

Gambia — Nutrition Field Working Party houses
at Genieri — 1948

two miles wide) to Balingho for a guide. On the way back the packing loosened so I went flat out for the creek, got her onto a mudbank, rammed the anchor on dry land and settled down to repack the gland nut. After that — 4.0 p.m. — I had 'brunch' and arrived back very tired and without soap, for I had run out and there was none to be had in Bathurst.

The launch proved an asset and among the Africans who crewed for me on later trips to Bathurst was a man distinguished from his companions, in that venereal disease had so ravaged his sexual organ that it had entirely parted from its owner, leaving him with a healed stump less than an inch in length. Nevertheless he worked well and I knew him as a handy man in a small boat in a hostile sea. He and I found ourselves one evening, chugging before a west wind blowing up the funnel of the Gambia River mouth. Before nightfall we were in riverine calm, only hampered by patches of weed which were difficult to see in the moonlight until they fouled the propeller, making it necessary to lean over the stern to clean it before proceeding. After several such delays the propeller became too entangled to clear in the dark, so we anchored and turned in to sleep till morning.

Day dawned and a warm sun shone down from a blue, blue sky. A perfect day only marred by the need to clear the propeller before we went on. Nothing disturbed the peace, not even a crocodile in all the four hundred yards on either side of the mangrove banks. By nature cautious, I scanned the waters carefully, for it is said that a croc must surface and so betray his presence every hundred yards or so. But the waters, brown-grey with silt washed by the retreating tide from the rice fields beyond the mangrove belt on either side, remained unbroken. Perhaps the crewman would like to go over the side to clear the propeller? But then a typically Fursean afterthought: was it right that a black man should precede a white where the latter hesitated to expose himself? 'Well . . . no. And while I am about it I may as well enjoy myself,' I thought. So I ran naked along the deck and, at the stern, leapt upwards into the air descending steeply in. A perfect dive, I felt. But surfacing, I was surprised to see how far from the boat my dive had carried me, and a second look, and it seemed further still. I realised that whereas the anchored boat remained immobile I was being carried on the stream towards the Gambia mouth. There was nothing to worry about; if I failed to make good the gap I could float on the outgoing current and clamber ashore on the next spit. Where the crocodiles would be. Fear lent me fins and I hastily made good the gap between the boat and me. The crewman, less cumbered with Fursean ethos than I, had remained aboard, and as I came level with the stern he reached over and heaved me in.

Housebuilding was going well by the end of March, despite my having to leave the work often in order to pay men for cutting mangrove poles or assess the value of grass brought in and so on, and to work in the dispensary. Later, a skilled plasterer turned up seeking work, and tired of living in utter chaos, I set him to work to finish my house and to make one of the round houses into a temporary office with barred windows and a padlocked door, so that I could move the saws, braces, trowels, buckets etc. and the stationery out of my bedroom. My new office was functioning by the end of the month and I celebrated by doing the month's returns and paperwork in it.

The roof trusses and ridgepole were up on the new house too. I enjoyed putting up roofs, it was high up and cool and fun handling the big, unwieldy timbers with inadequate tackle. For the roof timbers the carpenter cut two faces of the poles so that they roughly morticed together and then bored a hole through both and drove a bamboo peg through.

In Bathurst I had been able to negotiate for a lorry to replace Juggernaut whose dynamo had failed, and Rowntree of the PUD drove it up for me. It was a dream to drive after Juggernaut, but it went to my heart to see how the driver drove her. And to her heart too — on one trip to fetch mangrove poles and grass she boiled at him which she did not do at me. Rowntree also gave me advice on fitting the water drums to lead into the baths and showed me a good contrivance at his house for getting water out of a well, which I hoped to copy. He lived at Jenoi, near the Agricultural Officer in charge of the rice farm, who was to work with us on swamp reclamation, and he taught me a number of useful dodges.

Hoping to learn how to do gland puncture as a means of diagnosing sleeping sickness I paid a short visit to a leprosy survey[(4)] which was settled near YBK and on my return gathered up the threads again and got things under way for the final spurt before the girls came out. Fortunately their arrival had been delayed. We needed a kitchen fireplace, so I made a clamp of bricks and burnt it, but was not pleased with the product, though I got enough bricks for my purpose, and we finished the plumbing for the girls' bath. Then I paid the labour for work done in my absence and dealt with a puzzling case of a man who could not pass urine.

At the end of April I drove down to Bathurst. I had finished the girls' houses on time and had become a familiar figure in the countryside. Now the work of the Survey proper could begin.

The Agronomist and the Dietician arrived in Bathurst at the beginning of May; I had met both the young women briefly in England when they had been appointed by Platt. The Administrator, who had been interviewed and engaged after I left, came to the Gambia some weeks later. In the event he turned out to have a flair for education so he concentrated on that and I continued with much of the administration.

> 'Life has been full of adventures.' I wrote to my wife on returning to Genieri with the girls. 'I rose at 6.0 . . . picked up the girls, and away. About 3 miles on the road it suddenly occurred to me that although I had seen that all loads were out of my room, I had not actually seen the cashbox (£250) on to the lorry. So we looked and behold it was not there. So we went back very fast to the *Lufthansa* house and it was not there either. So I took the day watchman to the Police station and scoured the land for the nightwatchman who was by then off duty. Both knew *nothing* about it! I phoned for a European policeman from Bathurst and as soon as he arrived at the Police Station we went to the *Lufthansa* and on the way one of our boys came to say the box was found. It was lying at the bottom of the cliff outside the house. Someone had had a good hack at the lock but failed to open it . . . We then went to Brikama (30 miles) had breakfast with the Halls (Veterinary Officer), on to Kassang, lunch with Gamble (an Anthropologist), back here by 6 p.m., where Eddy (deputy DMS) and Barrett, the Labour Officer, were installed. Eddy was fairly shaken by our bush conditions, I think, but the two girls were grand, they were both glad to have homes of their own and took to conditions like ducks to water, and regarded the whole thing as a grand adventure.'

As usual, on my return from Bathurst, I had to deal with a mass of odd jobs, working through accounts and so on, and measuring up the amount of work done by the plasterer. We all went over to Jenoi at lunch time and walked over the rice station beneath a red hot sun with the Agricultural Officer, and then had a long talk on the matter of getting out a report on reclamation of 200 acres of swamp for next year. The next day I took them to the western side of the swamp, to the villages of Jomar and Jassobo and to Toniataba in the middle, with a view to selecting a good spot for survey there and to see what the chances of reclamation were at that end. I fixed for some houses to be built there as it seemed suitable for survey and we came back as far as Kaiaff and measured a bit of swamp there and laid plans for the scope or scale of our survey. The Agronomist, I told my wife, was 'a bit difficult through trying too hard.' She and the Dietician were immensely keen to get on with their respective jobs, but with no experience of Africa had no idea of the difficulties they would face.

The next day, in the heat of the afternoon, we mapped out a bit of Genieri and took the family relations of the inmates of one yard. It gave them a better idea of the work involved as hitherto they had been 'talking gaily of plotting whole villages'. We then interviewed a mass of illiterates who wanted to be recorders (agricultural and dietetic) and who would write in Mandinka. It all took much time but I felt we were slowly getting under way. The 10th May was a day of 'much measuring, mapping and God knows what', I wrote home:

> 'Rowntree came for lunch and fixed a bit more bathroom for me and after lunch we went to Pakali Nding where I got the chief all set for having a little bit of his village surveyed. Then to Toniataba to do the same. Then back and checked up some of the work of the Mandinka writers. Then supper. I am writing this by a horrible light so will stop now . . .'

My letters recording events between the 10th May and the 20th August are missing but during this period we made the switch from our original plan for reclaiming swamp land for growing rice to groundnut production, for reasons which I will explain in the next chapter.

When the rains began in May/June we three spent many hours charting, day by day, the time spent by farmers on various activities, from clearing and sowing the land to weeding, bird scaring and (ultimately) harvesting the crops. I, too, performed these activities, by hand as the peasant did, and likened them as nearly as I could to activities with which I was familiar and of which the energy expenditure per unit of time was already fairly well known, and had been reported in published work, such as walking, sitting, resting, sawing and the like.

As a check upon these estimates the intake of various foods was weighed and recorded over a continuous period, and we were able to make a comparison of energy intake and expenditure. When over the same period energy expenditure was observed to exceed energy intake, weight should fall, and by weekly weighings under constant conditions it was demonstrated that weight did fall. Before dawn two stalwart Gambians and I visited the huts of a sample of villagers with a weighing machine and, waking the inmates, persuaded them to urinate and then weighed them. This technique was evolved and passed on to us by Platt from his Nyasaland Survey. From the energy balance it was possible to predict what the weight loss or gain might be and these predictions were confirmed by the weight records.

There was, as Platt had observed in Nyasaland, a 'hungry season' during which weight was lost, co-incident with the tasks of clearing the land and weeding. As the various crops were harvested weights rose once more and it became difficult to record intakes as people were taking odd snacks throughout the day, but body weight returned more or less to normal. Even so, they lived a lean life with the leanest period just before harvest when they most needed their full strength.

This 'hungry season' was at the heart of the problem of peasants working with hand implements and without beasts of burden to do the heaviest tasks. In theory, at least, the best of the farmers, or those with most foresight, might have started the 'hungry season' with sufficient reserve of food to carry them through to harvest time and so reverse what would otherwise be a perpetual vicious circle: of tired and underfed men, inadequately caring for crops which, because of inadequate care, yielded in their turn inadequately, and thus to yet another 'hungry season'. As in Nyasaland, the phenomenon of improvidence and lack of foresight was largely responsible for this, for the harvest was a season of feast and jollification which left them with too little of food to see them through the spells of heavy work to come. Yet life was hard, as we well knew, having worked alongside them, and if we could provide them with tractor power at least for the period of their hardest work, they, or the best of them, might be able to reverse the vicious circle and get on top of their environment.

During our Survey of the villages we found how important was the clan system in Gambian society and the following illustrates its influence. My interpreter and I were once walking down a path into Genieri village. A pleasant young woman approached with a water jar on her head. *'I kontong?'* (Your clan?) she asked. *'Sane'* from the interpreter. 'My uncle' — and she bobbed a little curtsy without upsetting the jar, and went on. 'You're not a *Sane',* I said quietly, when she was out of earshot. 'I know', he said reluctantly and furtively, 'but almost everyone in this village is, and unless you are, or say you are, you can't buy any food in this village.'

From time to time we met in our work further indications of the influence of the clan system. One man stole three sheets of corrugated iron and was caught crossing the River Gambia with them in his possession. My proposal to prosecute him caused obvious distress. 'You see, he is one of *us.'* The prosecution was not proceeded with, for the sake of peace, and it seemed that somewhere and somehow sufficient sanctions were applied to act as a deterrent, at least for the time being. But clearly accidents of birth could not indefinitely confer immunity from consequences of crimes. Also problems of hardship and of money economics were just beginning to impinge on Gambian society. A money lender or lender of food was understandably embarrassed if he had to press men of his own clan for repayments, and he was therefore reluctant to enter into such commitments at all. The two main questions that we would need to resolve (or to be more precise, would have had to resolve had we been permitted to continue) clearly related to the ability of the clan system to persist, and to offer advantages in the face of economic or similar serious stress, or whether it acted as an impediment to the adaptation of society to such stresses.

Time was needed, in terms, not so much of the calendar, but of time to observe behaviour in response to the phenomenom of mechanisation and its successful grafting onto native society but time, I began to realise, was not going to be given us and the pressure to move faster was to increase.

Notes and References

(1) 'Contributions to a socio-economic survey of the Gambia' Gamble D.P. Research Dept., Colonial Office, London 1949. From the *Report* of the Department for 1948: 'the concentration of sulphur iron salts in the mangrove soils means that impoldering to enable the land to carry machines would be very dangerous indeed . . . While they are subject to tidal inundation the iron salts remain to a depth of about 12 inches and do not interfere with rice cultivation. Should they be brought to the surface oxidation would produce such a low PH value that all forms of life would be exterminated.' Gamble concludes: 'One is therefore confronted with an enormous problem for which there is no easy and obvious solution.'

(2) With ten years and a world war between them, the Nyasaland and Gambian Surveys and Development Units show differences in almost every respect. The Nyasaland Survey team consisted of two experienced Chinyanja-speaking Colonial Service officers (one medical and one agricultural) and one anthropologist, all three with knowledge of local conditions; and of three members who knew little or nothing of Africa, Platt, Jessie Barker, Miss Owen, and later Geoffrey Herklots. A house was put at the disposal of the team at Chintembwe, some distance

from the hill village chosen for the Survey and in a healthy climate. The anthropologist lived separately, as did the married Agricultural officer, and the medical officer was stationed at Kota Kota near the Survey village of Kasamba. Some of the team also camped regularly in the two villages and in Biwi's, the third Survey village in the foothills, so that most members were able to get away from one another, an important point for a group of people living in an isolated district. A secretary was employed for the paperwork and accounts and the housekeeping was undertaken by Mrs Platt. The district was served by an all-weather road, transport for all was available, there were frequent visitors and there was some opportunity and time for exercise and a certain amount of recreation.

Originally the Survey was to take a year — in fact, it was extended to eighteen months. A progress Report was sent home after six months and, though unfinished, a final Report was delivered to the Colonial Office in 1940, though the Nyasaland Government was still asking for it twelve years later.

The Nutrition development Unit which followed the Survey was given a term of three years. It consisted of picked Colonial Service officers with the same background, and the Nutritional Investigator, Jessie Barker, who had by then spent over a year in the country. All the Unit members spoke *Chinyanja,* they all worked together as a team with a common aim and they were aware of many of the difficulties before they began, though these were exacerbated by the war.

The composition of the Gambian team was different from that in Nyasaland. The Colonial Service was very short of experienced officers, many of the younger ones had been killed in the war and the older ones were either nearing or had reached retiring age, therefore secondment of experienced men to the Survey and Nutrition Field Working Party from the Colonial Service was not practicable. On demobilisation, suitable men from the forces were either snapped up by other concerns or did not want to go abroad again so soon after the end of the war. Thus the members of the Gambian team were all strangers to each other and to the country and I was the only member of the team with an intimate knowledge of tropical Africa and of the Colonial Service. The war had been over barely eighteen months when I arrived in January 1947 and there were shortages of every kind in food, household goods, building materials and transport. My first task was to build the houses for myself and the team, as well as look after the health of the area, with no transport at first and in a very primitive area of swamp and bush. Each member of the team when they arrived four months later was highly dedicated, but none could speak *Mandinka* and each was motivated initially by a different aim: the dietician to weigh and measure whole villages, the agronomist to plough large areas, the administrator to teach his thousands. The work was made more difficult by the fact that we were required to submit frequent interim reports with no secretary to attend to the paperwork, that the housekeeping had to be done by a member of the team as well as her own work and that there was no time or opportunity for recreation outside the village of Genieri in which we lived.

Perhaps had we been given the eighteen months which were eventually allotted to the Nyasaland Survey, before having to begin the Research into Development programme, the team might have been welded into a coherent whole and worked together towards a goal understood by all, but we were too pressed for time and, as a result, too tired, to withstand the pressures put upon us.

(3) Miss Joyce Griffiths (now Mrs Joyce Doughty).

(4) *'The Ross Medical Survey'.* Dr Charles M. Ross of the Nigerian Leprosy Service was head of this Survey to assess the prevalence of leprosy and to gather information concerning other endemic diseases, helped by a lay worker employed by the British Empire Leprosy Relief Association.

Chapter 8

As I wrote in the last chapter, at some point during the period, May to August, it had become obvious to us and to the Agricultural Department that the problems connected with growing rice on a potential 200 acres of newly impoldered land were for the present too great for us to tackle, at least until the reasons for the crop failures in Sierra Leone were understood and some means of overcoming them discovered.[1].

The difficulties of tractor driving on un-impoldered swamp were told me by the Agricultural Officer. The Agricultural Department tractor driver had tackled too heavy a load and the tractor began to dig its way through the crust of mud. The driver's sole response was to accelerate, the track revolved faster and the tractor sank deeper into the crust, which had dried during the hours of low tide when the waters did not flood the surface of the rice land. With only a limited time to spare till the tide rose again, the Agricultural Officer started the motor slowly in gear until the pin which held the track together appeared at the surface at the rear end of the tractor. He then removed this pin and with his gang (and the motor stopped), he detached the entire caterpillar track and laid it on the surface and fixed it at the fore end. He himself then very slowly set the wheel in motion and the tractor rode up on the track, being halted near the front end. With his gang he then dug out the track behind and manually laid it over the wheel and fixed it once more to the front end of the track. The tractor, driven more carefully, then proceeded safely over the thin crust of mud which formed the surface of the swamp and reached safety on the higher ground at the edge of the swamp before the tide rose.

Having to abandon the rice scheme, we turned to our second string — the growing of groundnuts by mechanisation. Though this was cash crop and not a staple food crop we hoped that by making it possible to grow larger amounts it would bring a better diet[2] and greater prosperity to the villagers, ultimately through their own efforts, and so raise their standard of living. The Agronomist went home to order more machinery and on the 20 th August, I started 'chaining' the land we hoped to run the groundnut machines on. I explained the process to my wife:

> 'The chain is 22 yards long. Every 10 chains one digs a hole 2 ft. deep to see if there are underlying rocks, and at the same time makes a count of all the trees present in one square chain. I covered 120 chain lengths in about four hours, that is about a mile and a half. Slow work. In the afternoon, I did another stretch, about 95 chains. More important, I trained Mr E. D. N. . . in the art of chaining, so he can do it in future. It is the sort of job that suits him and he did it very well. I can't yet place him where I want him. He seems a good chap and a slogger at work, within certain narrow limits. He has, for example, no idea that it is not the thing for a Government social welfare officer to sell cigarettes and generally indulge in petty trade in his spare time. Most of his ideas are merely compilations of other people's ideas, and his reports bear no relation to his actions. His reports are full of windy talk of cooperatives and community spirit and so on; his actions are shrewd and efficient on a limited, earthy, scale. Once we find his niche he will do well, but in the meantime I have to rub it in to him . . . that the time is not ripe for Youth clubs, Young Farmers movements, and so on.'

Later, when the time came to work out how the tractor was to do its ploughing, we asked for the services of three elders to advise us as to whose land should be ploughed, and how much, because a certain amount of rights to land would have to be taken into account although it had not been put under cultivation during the immediately preceding years. These elders needed to be representative of their village, and we arranged that out of a short list of candidates each should be represented by a tangible symbol, such as a groundnut or other seed or fruit; that one such symbol should be placed privately in my hand by the head of the 'yard' and the totals for each candidate counted up at the close. The three with most symbols lodged with me should be appointed. The dietician acting as observer noted that the voting proceeded largely along social (clan) lines. The *Alkali* (headman) who was not a *Sane* received very few votes.

Obviously this problem would need careful thought, when serious matters came to be decided. The choosing of these men to advise us, strangers, was fortuitously ideal for our purpose, because although it obviously was of interest and fairly important to the village it was not a life-and-death affair and we encountered no trouble subsequently because of the procedure.

When trials were made with the Fordson tractor, the Africans complained that the ridges it made were too high. I noticed that when the farmers were sowing onto our ridges this was done by the heavy wooden pestle used in pounding grain. On our powdery soil formed by the ploughshare, the pestle caused a deeper depression than when the ridges had been formed by hand hoeing, which merely inverted a slice of soil and weeds. As a result our groundnuts were planted deeper when land was ridged by machine than when ridged by hand. The fault of overdeep penetration of the planting pestle would, I think, have been prevented simply by fitting a horizontal collar (with one or two brackets). Whether it would then be shown that the groundnut shoots no longer broke surface a week or so later when planted on our 'high' ridges, I do not know. If not then the many differences between our mechanised ploughing and native practice would have had to be systematically investigated, including the relative difference in 'poverty' between the soils which the villagers lent to the agronomist.

Subsequently we discussed, first with the District Commissioner and the local Agricultural Officer, a project whereby the farmers would be offered, at a price, machine ploughing of one acre of land for every two acres that they had hoed. In this it would be necessary for them to hoe their previous acreage and to perform by hand the post-clearance tasks of sowing, weeding, bird-scaring, harvesting etc. but on a larger acreage than before (by some 50%). This residue of tasks was however lighter, and should be within their capacity, and it was likely that they would undertake it because only so would they have the advantage of a larger than usual run up to harvest (of their main cash crop). For the services of the tractor and its driver in this way, they would be asked to pay, in advance, £1.10s. per acre.

While planning these various stages I was, at the same time, trying to do my clinical work which included a paludrine experiment. This involved taking a sample of blood from each volunteer, who was given sugar as an inducement, but I wrote to my wife:

> 'I only got under way after a false start as I got no good out of my last lot of bloods, and so have to take them again which I shall do tomorrow, bribing them with much sugar. I shall also do their haemoglobins by Haldane's method. I took their temperatures the other evening and quite a lot of them were in the 98.5-99.8 region, old folk as much as young, so it may not be malaria. The only way to be sure is to give them a hearty course of paludrine and then compare with controls.'

Three days later I wrote:

> 'I spent the afternoon trying to round up my paludrine experiment people. Not much luck.

Ultimately the dietician suggested paying 3d for a full examination, and 1d for visits for taking the stuff, and the suggestion was well received, but two days later:

> 'I tried to do haemoglobins for my paludrine experiment but something went wrong with my gas generator so I had to pay them and send them back home. They are to come tomorrow. I will have a hell of a lot of them tomorrow, alas.'

My time had been so occupied since the arrival of the girls and the Administrator, in introducing them all to their unfamiliar work that I was only able to begin the main medical survey on the 26th September, that is, the full physical examination of the large sample in Genieri and the spot samples in the outer villages. I wrote my worries to my wife:

> '. . . (it) took me the whole day to do six people. No doubt I shall be able to speed it up a bit when I've got into the technique, but if I go at the rate of six daily, on a six-day week, then it will take about four months. In less than four months I shall be needed almost full time on the very difficult task of putting the machine business over. So I propose to try and rope in (Dr) Hadden to help me out. He is to be MO Middle River Division, so will be on the spot. I shall see Mackay (the DMS) this coming week and see what he thinks and then tackle Platt when he comes, which will I think be around October 14th. It was rather pleasant to be doing a clinical job again, but it would be more pleasant still to do a full time job as leader of this team. There's an awful lot of planning to do and I just haven't time to do it, as things are at present.'

In the same letter I voiced my anxieties about the work that the Administrator was doing:

> '. . . he is not quite at home. The trouble is, he is working on a somewhat bottlewashing job bar his education business, and his education is going through the mill in order to make it fit into the whole programme. He, I think, had rather thought of teaching his thousands to read, which is his strong suit and he's very good at it, while we are pressing him to teach his hundreds to read, write, do arithmetic, and understand something about agriculture and machinery. Also I don't help at the moment because I have a course to steer between what Govt. would like us to do in mass education and what we want done, and Bathurst is far away, so I can only postpone decisions . . .
>
> The other fly in our ointment is that the poorer paid bits of our Bathurst staff are going through a rough spell as food is short and mosquitoes plentiful, so that there is a falling off in health. But the harvest will be in in 5 or 6 weeks and so things will be better then. In the meantime, however, lean times are with us . . .

Unfortunately by October there was yet another fly in the ointment in the form of friction between the two girls and this erupted one lunchtime, until the Administrator tactfully diverted the conversation. I told my wife that fortunately these incidents

> 'occur more rarely at present, and should occur even less often when Platt has been and gone. I think we feel the survey hanging over our heads too much. Platt once did a survey and so he knows all about them. He will expect standards equal to his own even though he had double the staff and didn't have to build his houses, and lived on an all-weather road, and so on. The agricultural survey is, I think, as good, the diet survey is about the same, though the circumstances and way they feed make it difficult to compare. (In) their medical survey Fitzmaurice (though a good doctor) was no surveyer, and Platt

was more a lab. man than a clinician. The Dietician here has done an immense amount of work on the sociology. Even so, we all of us, myself included, fear Platt and what he may say or may try and do, and still more feel that we will, by December when the harvests are all in, know so much about the village that we can safely move onto development and *must*. There is one hell of a lot to do before next rains.'

We were all of us feeling oppressed by the amount of work. I had come across the Dietician in a state of deep depression: 'We can't get finished in the time', was all she said.

To add to my worries I accidentally discovered, to my astonishment, that rumours about my personal conduct were circulating in Fajara and elsewhere in the Protectorate. Being given a hint as to who was responsible I decided I must take strong and immediate action to stop them. I wrote to my brother Dick, to enlist his aid, and he wrote a 'solicitor's letter' to the person in question. I did not see the letter but was told by my other brother that it was a 'stinker' and as far as I am aware it had the desired effect.

We had heard that John Wakefield would be accompanying Platt in October and they both arrived on the 12th. The Tanganyika Groundnut Scheme was by then running into trouble and Wakefield was feeling the strain, though in Genieri we had heard little of it for we were cut off from the outside world. We had no radio, few newspapers and no time to read.

I went down to Bathurst to meet them and laid on a launch from Government to take them up river the same night. We started at 10.45 p.m. and arrived at Balingho about 12 hours later.

'Just before Balingho,' I wrote to my wife, 'we passed a big canoe going for Genieri creek so I bargained with the paddlers to take us, provided the launch would tow us to the Genieri side of the river. The (African) captain of the launch refused, he said his orders were to take us to Balingho and then return and that was what he was going to do. So we had to send the canoe off, and got to Balingho. I then started to negotiate with the captain of the Agricultural Officer's launch. *He* said he had orders not to shift except to take people to Sankwiya. So then I went back to the launch we came on and got on it and said if you go back you take me with you to report to your master . . . after some delay he felt impelled to take us across. We towed a canoe and got up our creek all right — at 4.0 p.m.

My passengers may have felt that my action was rather domineering but we could not be sure of getting up the creek on an outgoing tide. By the time we were up the creek the tide was beginning to ebb and Wakefield said that he realised we would never have been able to get up it had we left it any later.

'That was Sunday.' I resumed to my wife, 'On Monday we started discussions first of the Survey. Wakefield and I clashed frequently, particularly over the following issue . . . I had timed the date of 'popping the question' (of mechanisation) to the people of Genieri for December, after the machinery had come out. My idea was to show them exactly what the advantages and disadvantages of a tractor were, how it could plough much land but used up fuel (by rigging up a glass petrol feed from a long tube so that they could see it being used up) and how fuel spent in turning at the ends of each field was wasted money, and so they must pool their lands together and so on. I had also planned a very simple working agreement binding for 1 year only.

Wakefield (and Platt to some extent) asked for a start with the question popping *now,* (October) leading up to a charter binding for 3 or 5 years, setting out all the objects and principles of the scheme, which said they, would very likely form the subject of a leader in the Times! Talk about counting your chickens before they're hatched! There matters ended for the day.

The next day I opened the ball by saying that all our plans had been laid for December and that we had followed a careful series of conditioning steps over the past months; that they had had talks with the assembled people and must surely see that they were behind us, so that they had no grounds for fears on that count, and that here they were, two days out from England, ordering us to change about — and finally, that what they wanted was, not a leader for the party, but a wireless transmitting set to London, so that we could take daily orders. The sarcasm passed well over Platt's head, he replied that he could not lay his hands on a sufficiently powerful set and we must disabuse ourselves of that idea — and was quite disconcerted when I told him it was meant as sarcasm. Well apparently Wakefield had spotted it even if Platt had not, and after a brief defence, or disclaimer, he sat down, and the subject was never raised again.

But it left me feeling a bit Hitler-ish and it was not decreased by the fact that about half an hour later in the discussions the Agronomist announced that her principal anxiety about the scheme was that there was no plan, and that whenever she put anything forward which did not happen to coincide with my idea of how things should go I promptly squashed it. On the latter count I asked her to cite . . . and she was unable to. On the former I told the meeting that we concluded every meeting we had by preparing a timing sheet . . . she later attacked the Dietician fiercely on the matter of feeding people (our labour in particular) . . . I was however much helped by the Dietician and the Administrator who backed me through thick and thin. This was just as well, as I would otherwise have had my hand weakened in the further discussion. The whole trouble was that they, (Platt and Wakefield) are both visionaries, idealists (Wakefield of a far purer type than Platt; in conversation over a beer later Wakefield said to Platt in that joking voice that half veils a truth: 'You really are the most jealous man I have ever met' — and a dagger glance passed between the two.) When I try and get their feet on the ground they look at me pityingly as one of earthy nature. However, affairs became much more amicable on day 3, and except that they had posted so much extra staff to me (on paper) that the thing had become unwieldy, I had no great quarrel. Wakefield bore no resentment for the cracks I had had at him and I began to like him very much. He was ill when he arrived (overwork) and the change refreshed him. Once off his hobbyhorse he got down to some very hard practical details which pleased me. Platt also became much more useful. Wakefield diagnosed the Agricultural Officer very well, said that he should be welded into the team as a worker-out of seed and fertiliser trials, etc. rather than as a practical man, and I think he is right . . provided there can be an official healing of the breach at home, too, between the Agri. Dept. and the Nutritionists.

Then came the meetings in Bathurst with the local Steering Committee. Their hardheadedness brought my visionaries down nearer to earth. There was an obvious clash which left the locals rather apprehensive of the soundness of my two. This they (Platt and Wakefield) clearly felt, Platt especially. He had a go over things with me to-day, and had evidently sensed their feelings. He and I hammered out a working arrangement for the future which pleased me very well. We are to remain a comparatively light flexible body as before, devoting ourselves to the project of 'research into development'; any outside body which requires special lines of research must provide its own staff and do its own work, our only onus being to provide facilities: we are to have part time expert help on things like industrial psychology from men visiting us for short periods and part time help over long periods from people like the local District Commissioner and Agricultural Officer . . . The thing that pleased me most was that we are released from all this necessity of satisfying specialists on their pet subjects, to go for the main objective. Platt got more and more human as time went on, and I liked him more. He is satisfied with what we have done, I think. I do not think that anyone ever realises *what* we've done until he has been there a while and realised the difficulties of communications, supplies, raw Africans and so on. Our virtue lies in having established ourselves, rather than in any special job . . .

Wakefield has left for England, much refreshed and determined to hammer at things that end. He proposes to get Strachey (the Minister of Food) to send out a team of 'highpowered' experts to go into the rice question. (From that last sentence you get the tenor of the last week, he just says 'I will do this and that'. Generally, as a matter of fact, after an incredible amount of labour, he *does* do this and that, and more power to him, but his mind leaps forward overconfidently. But I must say I like him very much indeed; he is so sincere . . .) I was as rude as hell to him in the first days of the meeting, and he finished up by telling the world, including the Governor, how inspired he was by our work and how he wished he could bring his Tanganyika staff over to see what could be done simply by "a man and a boy" . . . I think his remark about Platt being a jealous man may have arisen from his insisting on his fair share of the credit for Wakefield's being inspired . . .'

I began another letter to my wife on the 21st October. The Administrator had burnt his leg against the exhaust of the motor bike and after leaving him to heal in hospital in Bathurst, I returned on the Vic 20:

'. . . she is an incredible old tramp which goes at about 4 knots . . . the two boys went off for lunch at one with strict injunctions to return at 2.0 p.m.; the ship left at 2.20 without them. The Vic was not over-comfortable when it came to sleeping that night. I spread my mattress on the (sloping hatch), as being the only place where it could be spread. On previous voyages many Africans had had the same idea, and they had left mementos, bedbugs I think, . . . To augment their anti-sleep effect, a great bell above my head rang out the hours. I beat them at about 4 but the crew staged a smart counterattack before dawn by taking down the awning above my head which roused me. I got off at Sankwiya, went along by lorry to Bob Rowntree's, and came on here on the back of a motorbike in the afternoon. The next morning I called the other two to discuss what had gone on at Bathurst . . . It is pretty clear from figures that we have been working out, that groundnuts may pay, but they may be rather a tight proposition. The right thing for Platt to do is to work for a ruling from higher up that, since large scale farming is coming into Africa, experiments must be carried out to find out the best way of putting it over, and that ours is one of them. . .

The trouble is that if that does happen, then it ceases to be a nutrition experiment and becomes a development experiment, and where is Platt? So he will have to fight with himself . . . Actually, if he were to overcome his self he would get back far more than if he hangs on and hangs on. Either other experiments of this nature will be brought in and because they start on a sound basis they will beat us, or we shall succeed, and be so fed up with the word nutrition that we almost repudiate it.'

By the end of October I had done some more medical survey and had 'been piling into the question of introducing these people to machinery. We have got to put up a working proposition to them in about one month's time, and we need to work out the ins and outs of it now. It is an interesting phase in our work and a lot will depend on it in the future. . .' I had hoped that there would be another committee meeting in Bathurst but 'Platt said "No, H.E. (His Excellency the Governor, Sir Andrew Barkworth Wright) and Palmer (the Director of Agriculture) will attend my committee meeting in London and I will round things off there". A pity, because the PUD have now slid out of building our (extra) houses and I have had to ask the acting Governor to deal with them. I would have preferred to deal with the Director in committee as before. However, I had my entire clan gathered to hear his words, so that we had things clear for the future, and so that the extreme vagueness and uncertainty of the future should be made clear to our Agronomist from the lips of the Master himself. So something was gained. Platt is more human than he was a year ago. For one thing he is succeeding. For another he is getting a dim idea of our difficulties and what our real aims and problems must be. Lord knows, existing as a body dependent on Government, but trying to move faster than Government in respect of building materials, etc. is hardship enough . . . Platt seems quite happy about progress to date and I don't think I shall be sacked. I think he realises that no one could endure such a hellish rough life as we lead, and on such a risky thankless job, except the people he has got on it. Certainly he could not get replacements at short notice. He may even realise that he can't hope to see the job succeed if he has a yes-man in charge of it (He quite certainly must realise that he has *not* got one in charge of it.) I think Wakefield did him a lot of good'.

Coming back from Bathurst I drove over a causeway, built over the bog and encountered a peasant leading a bull.

'The bull got restive and I edged away from him and got to near the soft earth on the side of the causeway. This was sodden with the very high spring tides and so down I went. By the time sundry lorries had tried to pull me out I had one wheel well in the bog and one half in. I got a lift home, and spent most of the next day getting out. Two punctures on the way back completed the picture.

My next task is to prepare the 3 months' progress report which is required of us now, as a result of Platt and Wakefield's visit. Platt wants details of any agricultural operations or medical jobs that can be presented as a completed entity. Which on thinking over it is a bit cool when you consider that he left Nyasaland 5 clear months after his survey was over without having completed any report at all and that now, 8 years later, it is still incomplete (and unpublished). However to all intents and purposes no portion of the survey can be presented as a nicely rounded entity this time, so they must be content largely with a review of the quarter's work from the administrative angle. I am engaged in working out a new approach to the social side of this mechanisation business. The Agronomist, after a mild resistance at the new idea, is coming round by degrees.

In November, the D 7 tractor arrived in Gambia together with the landing craft. At Bathurst, the landing craft was winched into the water, the D 7 was lifted out and placed in it and the landing craft beached itself, allowing the D 7 to be driven onto dry land to await the next stage of its journey. The Director of Agriculture had solved ingeniously the problem of getting it to Genieri by prospecting up-river until he found an ironstone spit capable of taking the tractor and giving access to the site of operations. A concrete ramp was built at the side of the spit, the tractor was put back into the landing craft, taken up-river and driven onto firm land and on to Genieri. We had an argument with the PUD who tried to offload the responsibility of driving it from the ship onto the riverbank on to us but we won the argument and a qualified mechanic was sent up to do it. We then awaited the arrival of a mechanic from England who had been appointed to look after all our machinery.

In December the Dietician and I attended a conference organised by the French in Bissao, Portuguese Guinea, south of Gambia. We both read papers describing the work of the Nutrition Field Working Party which aroused great interest. It was here that I awoke one night to find myself looking into the eyes of the hotel's chimpanzee which was allowed to roam loose. I had a routine in Africa, meticulously consistent, of putting my small possessions, spectacles, watch, cash etc. each in its own place at night and in the right order, so that on awakening I knew at once where they could be found. It stood me in good stead that night as I was able immediately to locate my small change, passport, etc. and other essentials and to protect them from his meddling fingers. This chimpanzee and I had also met during the day. It joined me in the lavatory, climbing over the top of the partition, when I was seated 'otherwise engaged', and after pulling many sheets off the toilet roll it gave a lively, if revealing, imitation of previous guests whom it had observed similarly engaged.

On a previous occasion in Gambia, when asleep in the moonlight on the concrete verandah outside Balingho Rural Dispensary, my nightly routine saved me from an embarrassing loss. I was woken by a peculiar chomping noise and knew at once what it was. A pariah dog had fished the small denture I wore out of the shoe in which I kept it at night for safety, and was speculatively mouthing it before deciding whether or not to swallow it. I knew, too, that my next move must be carefully planned, or I should end up running barefoot in pyjamas up the earth road, between the huts of Balingho, in pursuit of my teeth borne triumphantly between his own by this wretched creature. A sudden enough shock should startle him into dropping the teeth and bolting in terror. So after lying silent and immobile for a while I suddenly shouted 'WAAAH'. All went as I had planned and I rose, retrieved my teeth in the moonlight, washed them well in disinfectant, put them to soak in it till morning, and went to bed again.

My wife arrived just before Christmas with our two younger children, now aged 5 and 3, after we had returned from Bissao. There had been many difficulties to overcome before she set off. In February I had written:

> '. . . I think we could invent something about needing a typist to get you a priority. The Harragin commission report recommended free passages for children as well as wife but the sods here are trying to dodge that because they do *not* want children out. But I expect the Colonial Office will override them.'

Two weeks later it seemed both children *might* get free passages, if passages were available, and we agreed on her coming from December to March. The two boys had just begun attending a school (High Trees) near Horley, which looked after Colonial children during the holidays and our elder child was to be left there. He was now seven and we felt that were he to miss a term it would be a great handicap to him.

The air service to West Africa was liable to sudden and unheralded alterations due to the problems of dovetailing into the service being developed by France. In September I wrote: 'For the Lord's sake make sure your plane is all right. Book only to Dakar (French West Africa) if you like and I can meet you.' On October 1st: 'This damned change of air routes. I'll meet you at Dakar, never fear . . .' I was referring to the British South American Airways Corporation which had transferred its jumping-off point for the South Atlantic crossing from Bathurst to Dakar, and its sister Corporation, British Overseas Airways, which had abandoned the West coast routes in favour of direct flights across the Sahara from Tripoli to Nigeria and Gold Coast. Gambia was then served by a twice weekly service from Lagos to Dakar which was supposed to connect with the BSAAC service at Dakar and the BOAC service at Lagos. In the Gambia we heard tales of passengers stranded for as long as ten days in Dakar, unable to buy food because they had spent their £5 travel allowance and having to receive help from the British Consul.

In the UK my wife was told the planes connected and booked to Bathurst but on November 1st I wrote:

> 'Cancel the Dakar-Bathurst bit. It is terribly unreliable. Take all the £5 to pay for your visa or landing permit, or whatever it is. 110 francs. I will endeavour to get enough black market francs to see us through. They are 400 to the £1 instead of the official 200 so the joke is on the French not us. It is a lousy journey. This, v. important, from Platt — Get in the *back* of the plane. They are apt to try and stick children in front; the back is far less noisy and shaky. I have been wondering how best to cope with you that night. The plane trip is a tiring one and having the children won't help. But the French prices are wicked. Do you think, if I took up camp beds and blankets, you could bear to be driven out of Dakar until we find a quiet spot and then sleep in the lorry? If on careful enquiry I find that is a bad idea I will just get so many black market francs that we sleep in comfort in Dakar . . .'

But that plan was changed again:

> 'Now policy re meeting you. You arrive at some bloody hour in the night (at Dakar), get driven to the Transit camp, have to roust out sleepy native boys to give you bedding — they never seem to know that you are coming apparently. The plane on is due some time in the p.m. of the next day. Sometimes it says it is not coming and then comes after all and all the passengers have been told it is not coming and have gone bathing and either it tries to find them or it just goes without them. The only certain thing is that if they say it won't go before a certain hour it won't go *before* that hour. I will go to Bathurst and wait for you *there*. If word comes to Bathurst that the plane isn't coming I will by hook or by crook get up to Dakar to meet you . . .'

And changed again on the 17th:

> 'I have to go to Bissao in Portuguese Guinea, early next month . . . As soon as I am sure of the date of returning I am going to try to get a passage to Dakar to meet you there *if* there is no plane which connects direct with yours, as now seems likely. So, bloody though Dakar may be, at least we will be all bloody together . . .'

But on the 24th November it was back to the original plan again and for the last time on December 6th: I wrote:

> '. . . I have sent, in a separate envelope, some French francs. I know it is an appalling thing to do but it seems so grim that you might be stuck in Dakar, that I took the risk. I shall be relieved to hear that they have arrived all right. If you feel too bad a criminal to carry them, then just leave them behind; we can leave them till I return from next leave and I'll dispose of them then. The best thing to

do though is to carry them yourself against emergency, without declaring them at all, in some secret portion of your apparel. No one will search you. Your last letter said that you were applying for permission to take a larger LSD[(3)] out of the country. I doubt if you will get it, but even if you do I should not use my little packet for that, it might be traced. Anyway, they may be French West African currency and not ordinary French currency and thus arouse suspish (suspicion). I am going to Bissao on Monday but will be back without fail to Bathurst on the 17th. If they say the plane has broken down or anything I will then endeavour to drive up and meet you in Dakar. If I have not got there by the Saturday then come down here on the Saturday's plane . . . If you are still at Dakar on Saturday the reason why you should come on is that I may have a breakdown or the road may be impassable and I cannot communicate with you . . . we shall be staying with Dr Hadden and I will endeavour to arrange for us to stay a further day before going on to Genieri. I am carrying one camp bed but two nets, so we can all settle under them away from mosquitoes if by any weird chance I had to go up to Dakar and we broke down on the way back . . .'

My wife sat up the night before leaving, unpicking the hem of her coat and inserting the black market currency all the way round it. Terror at this illegal transaction made her imagine that not only did she crackle as she walked but that every official they met at the airport must suspect her, such is the power of a guilty conscience. They arrived at Dakar just after midnight and were driven to the transit camp outside the town without mishap, there to await the connecting plane. Nobody could say when it would arrive and as the second day dawned the row of vultures permanently perched on the wall outside the dining room, seemed to take on an evermore sinister significance!

The road out of the transit camp was hot and dusty and the children were too young to walk far; she dared not go in to Dakar in case the aircraft arrived. The few other male passengers in the camp spent their time in the bar and she had just decided to repack a suitcase in the evening and had spread all her things on the bed, while the children slept, when in burst the Agent: 'The plane leaves in 20 minutes' he announced triumphantly.

After Christmas the mechanic from England arrived. He proved to be young and energetic, ready to turn his hand to anything, and with a cheerfully uncomplicated character. He lived uncomplainingly in a one-roomed 'house' which had originally been built by me as part of the plan to house the African labour force.

A new toothed bulldozer blade for the D 7 was expected from England and at breakfast one day, shortly after the mechanic's arrival, a message came that the steamer, en route up-river, had off-loaded the bulldozer blade onto the bank for us. From its Lading notes I found it weighed 2¼ tons.

Since the mechanic had a job to do that morning, I drove with a gang to see what the problem of moving it was likely to involve. There lay the blade, a square, squat, double-bladed object with a set of iron teeth capable of fitting into its edge, the idea being presumably that these should scarify the land to a depth of about a foot, pushed by the D 7 tractor, to rip up roots.

The difficulty was to raise it a matter of 4 feet, and so get it onto the tractor trailer to carry it away. It was obviously beyond the capacity of the labour gang to do this. The landing stage was not supplied with a crane, but there were three 10-15 feet iron pipes *(whose* I did not enquire!) and a number of 2 × 2 inch square wooden staves. The gang cut for me a pole of black mangrove from a nearby stand, and I had brought with me a block and tackle and hawser. By a little digging the tip of the mangrove pole (some 10 feet long) was inserted, the hawser being lashed close to its insertion, the pipes were then lashed to form a tripod with the block at its apex, and the hawser looped through it and lashed to the mangrove pole. The entire gang sat on this pole and their weight was sufficient to raise one end of the blade a few inches, thus enabling a 2×2 inch square stave to be thrust beneath it. The pipes were then re-erected to form a tripod at the other end of the blade and the process repeated so that both ends of the blade were raised off the ground and in due course the blade rested, horizontally, about 2 inches off the ground (not quite 2 inches because the great weight of the blade caused the sodden soil beneath the rod to pack down somewhat). After repeating the whole process again at both ends, and inserting yet another rod at either end, the entire blade was raised about a further 2 inches. By repeating the process several times in the next hour the blade was lifted some 2 or 2½ feet from the ground, at which stage the entire Heath Robinson apparatus collapsed and we had to start again.

Ultimately the blade had been raised some three feet into the air, we therefore manhandled the trailer so that it stood free, dug a ditch behind each rear wheel and carefully manhandled it (now 'down at the starn') into these ditches. Even then, though the two ditches were so deep that the back axle was resting on the ground, the rear end of the trailer still stood just too high to be inserted below the bulldozer blade. I then accepted defeat, the sun being lower in the heavens than when I had started (about 3 p.m. I judged) and sent word for the mechanic to come with a further gang.

He arrived, and surveyed the problem as Napoleon might have done. There was a ring at the centre of the bulldozer blade through which he passed the hawser, attaching one end of it to the trailer and the other to the Fordson Major tractor at the front end of the trailer, started the tractor up and drove it forward. What happened next will, I am sure, be crystal-clear to the reader! The force of the tractor pulled the blade forward, but simultaneously the hawser, dragged through the ring through which it had been passed pulled the trailer backwards so that everything closed up abruptly and, before the blade had time to fall, that gap had closed. There was a mighty noise, of the blade crashing onto the end of the trailer and of my 2×2 inch staves scattering, the hawser broke, and the Fordson Major tractor, thus released, went bucketing across the landing stage, to be restrained by a quick pull on the brakes. We hastily lashed it in place and sat all the labour gang on the front of the trailer to restrain any urge it might feel to rear in the air due to the great weight at its other end. As we drove home in the car we passed the blade, trailer and all, pulled by the Fordson Major and proceeding over the uneven road with a curiously duck-like waddling gait, due presumably to its bearing great weights at either end but none in the middle. I slept the sleep of exhaustion — and of relief — that night.

Early next morning, while I still slept, the mechanic rose, and with the D 7 tractor, carefully towed the trailer, with its burden still lashed in place, until the blade lay underneath a huge forest tree which he knew as having a strong, horizontal limb. Unlashing the hawser he passed one end through the ring, over the limb of the tree and to the winch of the D 7 tractor standing near-by. Then by raising the blade and carefully advancing the D 7 tractor and tightening the winch at the same time, he eventually reached the stage where the bulldozer blade hung precisely between the two arms of the D 7 tractor, in readiness to receive it. At this stage he saw that the blade which had been sent out was not of a size appropriate to the tractor! At no point did it fit nor could it be made to fit.

When I woke the mechanic told me the bad news. I was not too perturbed, since we had, months before, felt that the D 7 tractor was something of a white elephant, and had based our plans (and performed our field trials) with the Fordson Major as our most powerful piece of equipment for use in the field. This, in our experience and observation of its performance, and from our knowledge of the clearance problems we must face, gained from the 'chaining' of the land, meant that we would be wise to limit our programme to 200 acres. It might reduce the degree to which we were able, by means of the D 7, to insure against unexpectedly heavy individual problems of bush clearance, of roots and tree stumps, but Mr E. D. N . . . had not reported anything particularly ominous.

At our meeting with Platt and Wakefield in October, however, it must have become obvious to them that the Agronomist and I were not going to manage to work together and Platt then had to decide which to retain in the long term. Her criticism that we had no overall plan undoubtedly touched on a weakness, arising out of the need to put definite proposals to the Gambian farmers with too little experience of the economics of mechanisation in the African bush; and, more specifically on how mechanisation could be of genuine use to them and in relation to which agricultural tasks throughout the groundnut year. It was obvious that every operation, whether heavy or light, could in theory involve running at least once over the entire acreage — which would be expensive.

As I have told, I eventually put forward to the local administrative and agricultural officers in committee the proposal that we should restrict ourselves, initially, to doing the first clearance ploughing by machine, at a price for each grower, on a scale rather more than was at present done by him by hand. Each farmer would then do by hand the succeeding operations of groundnut cultivation — sowing, pest-scaring, weeding, harvesting and marketing. This would relieve him of the heaviest work of all, which used formerly to be done during the hungry season when weight loss was greatest and the energy debt greatest. Since all the subsequent tasks were lighter a rather larger acreage than hitherto could then be farmed. By restricting the acreage mechanically ploughed for him, to the amount which he had previously farmed, he would not be confronted by more than he could keep hand cultivated up till harvest. We calculated as nearly as we could the cost per acre of this one operation. We judged that no supervision by us would be needed during subsequent operations, since the reward, for good or bad work, would be reflected in the price obtained for his crop. The local Government officers accepted this plan.

A few weeks after Christmas, I was asked by Platt to comment on a typed and unsigned proposal for cultivation of a considerably larger acreage than I had proposed; I recall no mention of what machinery was proposed nor of trials made of its performance. I said that in my view it was impracticable and not in accord with the principles that I was following of involving the villagers in the project of mechanisation. Sooner than have anything to do with it I would prefer to resign. In this I was supported by the Dietician who was also prepared to resign. I do not know who was the author of this proposal but it contained no details of any basis of relationship to the villagers, and whereas our proposals were for 'group' use of machines, this smacked of a 'plantation' project.[(4)] Platt seemed disconcerted and suggested that we should put both plans before the Gambia Government's Steering Committee. This body backed me and the smaller acreage.

It is an indication of the thoroughness of the scrutiny and of our thoroughness, that our decision to abandon cultivation of one of the minor cereal crops was closely questioned on the grounds that it was farming practice the world over to grow a variety of crops as an insurance against one or other crop failing. To this the Dietician was able to reply that its overall energy contribution only amounted to about one day's energy supply for the village. I pointed out that there were advantages to simplifying the proposals for mechanisation where it could be done without loss of energy yield. Also the Genieri farmers could see for themselves the nature of the service for which they were being asked to pay and no pressure on them would be needed — they could take it or leave it — but in the outcome they would be relieved of the heaviest task of the agricultural season.

When Platt later asked me whether we still proposed to resign, I said: 'Of course not', for the Steering Committee had given us everything we wanted. Platt said nothing, but he had been put in an impossible position and in due course I got a letter from him asking for my resignation. I had, he wrote, failed to keep my team together. A reasonable move since the over-riding problems ahead of us were agricultural, but I raised the issue with the Governor of the Gambia, who replied that Platt had the right to do this, as he bore the responsibility for the success or failure of the scheme.

So, with my wife and children, I left Genieri in March, 1948, staying for a few days at Government House, before our ship sailed for England.

The Genieri Nutrition Field Working Party closed down two years later, having failed to plough the increased acreage. The Agricultural Department took over: 'accepting responsibility for continuing a modified experiment to encourage group farming with a minimum of mechanical equipment.'

This quotation from the *Colonial Report on the Gambia 1950 and 1951* begins:

> 'Experimental work carried out by the Field Nutrition Working Party (sic) under the aegis of the MRC served to underline the danger of too rapid and extensive mechanisation of agriculture in this territory . . .'

So ended my pursuit of the *'ignis fatuus'* of true self-rule under the British Colonial system in Africa as, disillusioned, I left the Colonial Service, aged 39, and from the sidelines of a new career in the (then) Ministry of Health in London, I studied, as a spectator, the collapse of the huge commercial schemes in Gambia and other parts of Africa. The Gambia Egg Scheme, approved by the Colonial Development Corporation Board in 1948, which had been given to understand (by whom?) that sufficient feeding stuffs could be grown locally. The Board advanced £825,000 before the Egg Scheme was closed down in 1951, after 30,000 laying hens had died of fowl typhoid; the fiasco of the East African Groundnut Scheme, costing *£35,000,000,* from which John Wakefield was dismissed, two years after I left Gambia; the Nyasaland Tung Scheme, with its expensive housing and bulldozer teams from outside the country; the Nyasaland Rice Scheme, begun without adequate control of the water supply, its over-mechanisation and general hurry under the Colonial Development Corporation management, with a huge depot of machinery and stores like that of the Groundnut Scheme at Kongwa in Tanganyika; all these and many others at a gigantic cost to the tax-payer.

What was the fundamental cause of these failures? What madness was this that permitted millions to be risked without adequate tests? I can only suggest that it arose out of two developing processes. First, a massive swing to Labour in 1945, reflecting a revulsion, mounting during the war, against the old order and leading to a new and inexperienced Government being elected.

Secondly, a general discontent at food shortages, which so far from ceasing at the end of the war, became actually worse owing to Britain's altruistic diversion of foods to European countries, whose peoples had suffered severely and were worse off then we. The new Labour Government was under pressure to show that they were doing *something* and, as each Government has perhaps only five years in office before the Oppostion takes its place, a proposal for a massive agricultural project to supply the British housewife with more margarine was put forward without sufficiently critical examination. This was the Tanganyika Groundnut Scheme.

Criticism there was. The head of Rothamstead Chemistry Department (W. M. Crowther) and the Principal of Wye College (D. Skilbeck) made a number of comments — that 500 lbs of groundnuts per acre might be more realistic than the 750 lbs to the acre estimated (originally 850 lbs), that the rainfall evidence was doubtful, that implements used in USA for bush clearing might not be best for Africa and they urged that small trials be made over scattered areas, that the plan be flexible and *the people must be in on the planning.*[(5)] These suggestions were ignored.

During the war millions of pounds had been spent on men and machines and after the war many thought that all food problems could be solved by spending more millions on huge commercial undertakings in Africa — millions of pounds, millions of acres, millions of tons of produce, nothing seemed impossible so long as it was big. By contrast, our non-commercial, cautious approach at Genieri appeared puny, petty, penny-wise, pound foolish. The basic principle which governed our scheme was to incorporate it into village life, not to destroy the village structure, to render the structure more adaptable with a view to genuine self-rule in the long term, for, to repeat the quotation: 'the people must be in on the planning.' Not to embark on anything grandiose until it had been preceded by a small-scale trial in the field, both from the point of view of its soundness, agriculturally and commercially, and to test whether it could be introduced into the existing native social structure without disrupting it.

In my view, Platt was carried away by the massive scale of the commercial scheme being launched on the other side of Africa and sub-consciously impatient with our apparently slow approach via pilot field experiments, deliberately kept small so long as they were sufficiently large to indicate the answers to the questions with which we were pre-occupied. I was on a totally different wave-length from him, with his web of high-sounding international scientific Committees, and never evoked a response. When a grander plan emerged for doubling the acreage — perhaps his? I never knew — he clutched at it and brushed aside the original objective. By the end of my time in Gambia, in fact, we were working towards quite different goals and our team was split between the two.

After my dismissal I, at least, emerged with benefit from my contact with Platt. I had learnt much, both about life and about the science of nutrition, which I would not have done had I remained an ordinary medical officer in Nyasaland, and which enabled me to become free of the then Colonial Service and to pursue a new career. We had our clashes but I must in fairness acknowledge my indebtedness.

By 1956, one at least of the lessons in Africa had been learnt. In his revised African Survey (1957), Lord Hailey writes: '. . . practically every project since (the Groundnut Scheme) initiated in tropical Africa has been exploratory or — to adopt the term now in common use — a "pilot scheme"'. But the lesson had been learnt too late, for within the next decade the Wind of Change had blown through Africa and, in the life of that Continent, a new chapter had begun.

Notes and References

(1) See Note 1, Chapter 7.

(2) Groundnuts are valued as a foodstuff and the oil for domestic purposes; it is said that a more extended use would remedy deficiences in native diets; The plant acts as a soil renovator and the haulms are a valuable addition to the fodder supply in mixed farming. (Hailey 1938)

(3) In those days LSD meant pounds, shillings and pence not drugs!

(4) 'Group' farming. The cultivators do not necessarily act as a collective group. It aims at settling independent cultivators in supervised groups, or providing group services (usually machinery) to farmers already in occupation of the land.
'Plantation' system. A term mostly confined to those undertakings which involve the large scale employment of non-native capital and management. (Hailey 1957. pps 911 & 980)

(5) Quoted in the Groundnut Affair by Alan Wood. p. 48. My italics.

POSTSCRIPT

The final chapter of the book ends abruptly but my husband died before he was able to revise the last few pages. As they show the direction of his thoughts I have left them as they stand. I also include below a paragraph written by the mechanic from our Gambia days, knowing that my husband, a most modest man, would never have consented to this in his lifetime:

> 'As it is always difficult for an author to give information which may seem to be self-glorification, I have asked for my impressions of the events of one morning in the Gambia to be included. It was the occasion of the departure of Dr Berry from the Unit that he had been running in a small isolated and (in the view of some people) unimportant village. At that time I was a very raw and new member of the team but I will never forget the trip in a lorry from our compound to the river bank to catch the river steamer on the way back to England. The distance was several miles through sparsely inhabited bush but all the way along the sandy track our lorry had to make its way through groups of local people who had come to see this man off and perhaps to say in some way, their thanks for all that he had done for them. Since that time I have worked for many years in different parts of Africa but I have never seen anything like this. A road normally with one or two passers-by now crowded with his friends. It made me feel that if I was ever fortunate enough to get even a small proportion of the number of people to see me off when I went home I should then feel that perhaps all my efforts had been worthwhile.'

Veronica Berry
4, Church Farm
Colney
Norwich NR4 7TX

BIBLIOGRAPHY

British Central Africa — Sir Harry *Johnston*. Methuen, London 1897.

A Handbook of Nyasaland — Compiled by S. S. *Murray*. Published by the Government of Nyasaland for the Crown Agents for the Colonies, 4, Millbank, London, 1932.

An African Survey — A Study of Problems arising in Africa South of the Sahara. — Lord *Hailey,* Oxford University Press, London 1938.

An African Survey — As above, revised, 1956. O.U.P. London 1957

The Nyasaland Nutrition Survey 1938-40 — (Unpublished). Human Nutrition Department, London School of Hygiene & Tropical Medicine, Keppel St., London, WC1E 7HT

Nyasaland Nutrition Unit 1940-1943 — As above.

The Gambia — Colonial Annual Reports. HMSO 1946, 1947, 1948, 1949, 1950, 1951.

The Groundnut Affair — Alan *Wood*. The Bodley Head, London, 1950

Nyasaland, The Land of the Lake. — Frank *Debenham*. HMSO. London 1955

The Story of the Rhodesias and Nyasaland. — A. J. *Hanna*. Faber & Faber, London, 1960.

Lugard — The Years of Authority 1898-1945 — Margery *Perham*. Collins, London, 1960

As I Recall — Lord *Boyd Orr*. MacGibbon & Kee, London, 1966

African Renaissance — Leonard *Barnes*. Gollanz, London, 1969.

Lake Malawi Steamers — R. A. *Cole-King*. Ministry of Local Government, Dept. of Antiquities, Government Printer, Zomba, 1971

Malawi — The History of a Nation — Bridglal *Pachai*. Longman Group Ltd., London 1973

Banda — Philip *Short*. Routledge & Kegan Paul, London, 1974

Useful Plants of Malawi — Jessie *Williamson*. Montford Press, Limbe, Malawi, 1974

Heaven's Command. An Imperial Progress — James (Jan) *Morris*. Faber & Faber Ltd. London 1973

Pax Britannica. The Climax of an Empire — James (Jan) *Morris*. Faber Paperbacks, Faber & Faber, London. 1975

Farewell the Trumpets. An Imperial Retreat — James (Jan) *Morris*. Penguin Books, England. 1979

INDEX

NKHOTAKOTA
DC Hosp TCt PO RH Mkt PS TC Miss Schs
MALENGA CHANZI
Kajontha
Daniel
Chivwamila
Kasichi
Katalima
KAPELULA
Bua
Rapids
Msupadzi
Ungwe Mkt
Chiwaula Mkt
Kasamba
Liwewe
Chanzi TCt
Kachuma
Chanika
Malenga
Holding Ground
Chisoti Sch
Chiputula
Sasani Sch
Sasani Market
Thandwe
Sani Mkt
Sani 837
Sani Sch RH
Chamkoma
Ozi
M10
D207
S33
Mbonekela 736
NKHOTAKOTA GAME RESERVE
Chipata 1638
Game Camp
Dwali
Nachiwale
Funga
Kazombe
Campasani
Nkhongo Market
Lake Mdila
Mbambara
Phwetekele
Nkhongo 586
MALENGA CHANZI
Chia PA H Unit School
Mtanga TC Mkt
Chia Lagoon
Namkwate
Chongole Market School
Nafenanji
Likoa
Chabwazi
Ngombe 1064
Mbobo
Mankaka School
Kazomba
S54
Malomo TCt TC PA Sch H Unit Market
Mankhalalo School
Mpasa 1418
Charunche School
Mkweche
Chigaduwe
Mawiri Sch
Kavula Hill
Mpalo
Market
Mtongo
Cheko 1162
Mtsile TCt
Msumba Mkt Sch
Chatumbi
Chaunga
Malusa Market
Kajaliza
NKHOTAKOTA
Lifulizi
Ngumbwe
Market
Mapala
Chingole
Zidyana 509
Zidyana Market
Msamala
Khwada